PMP®/CAPM® EXAM PREP: A Basic Guide to Activity-On-Node and Critical Path Method

Front Image © Sashkinw | Dreamstime.com

Dedication Photo © 2011 Jayanta Das Purkayastha

ATTENTION CORPORATIONS, UNIVERSITIES, COLLEGES, AND PROFESSIONAL ORGANIZATIONS. Quantity discounts are available on bulk purchases of this guide. For information, please contact the publisher.

Published in the United States by Booklocker.com, Inc., Bangor, Maine.

Printed in the United States of America on acid-free paper.

Booklocker.com, Inc.

2011

First Edition

PMP®/CAPM® EXAM PREP: A Basic Guide to Activity-On-Node and Critical Path Method

By

Jayanta Das Purkayastha

Dedication

To my mom, sister, and wife for their love, patience, and support.

"Love is like a tree, it grows of its own accord, it puts down deep roots into our whole being."
--Victor Hugo

Acknowledgements

It may seem as an easy task to write the acknowledgement section but trust me that it is not. The challenge for me is whether I can really do justice to the efforts of many who have contributed directly and indirectly to my efforts. At best, I sincerely hope to express gratitude and thankfulness, and note their contribution as a humble recognition, but by no means trivial.

First and foremost, I must note the enormous contribution of my mom, Monica Das Purkayastha, whose tireless and almost seemingly superhuman efforts provided me the guidance I needed in life. My zest for learning and appetite for knowledge was planted in me at a much younger age than I can actually remember. Thank you, mom!

Knowledge is dynamic and constantly forever evolves as our own understanding and awareness grow. I thank my sister for standing by me through hard times and constantly providing me with information and different approaches that otherwise I may have never come across. Among her many talents, the one that helped me most in this effort was her ability to dig up treasure-troves of information on the internet.

This acknowledgement would be incomplete if I were not to mention the most important lady in my life—my wife. She is an amazing embodiment of energy, intellect, and foresight. Her countless feedback and suggestions, and most importantly her support and patience make endeavors like this possible for me.

I would like to thank Eloisa Haimann, whose mentorship and long experience in project management opened the door for me into Project Management. Our professional and intellectual discussions on different topics in project management regarding its practice, best practices, and pitfalls immensely helped in molding and directing my own study and intellectual inquiry. In addition, I thank her for reviewing multiple revisions and providing valuable feedback.

Finally, many thanks to the copyediting work done by Anna Editing & Proofreading which helped in preparing this guide for publication.

This work, like countless others, is based on the work and knowledge of many scholars and practitioners in this field, whose books, blogs, and articles have immensely contributed to my own understanding and knowledge.

Table of Contents

What This Guide Is About   xiii

What this Guide Is Not About   xiii

Who This Guide Is For   xiv

Feedback   xiv

Section 1: Get the Basics   1

Summary 3

Introduction 3

Understanding Basics of an Activity: Building Block of Activity-On-Node (AON) 6

Understanding Basics of Precedence Diagramming Method (PDM)/ Activity-On-Node (AON) Diagram 15

Section 2: Critical Path Method   23

Understanding Critical Activities and Critical Path 25

Determine Critical Path in a Project Network Diagram 26

Section 3: Critical Path Analysis of AON using CPM   31

Determining Activity Early Start and Early Finish: Forward Pass 33

Determining Activity Late Start and Late Finish: Backward Pass 37

Section 4: Solved Examples   43

Example 1 45

Example 2 48

Example 3 52

Example 4 56

Example 5 61

Section 5: Conclusion   67

Benefits of Using AON and CPM 69

Practice Exercises   71

Further Readings   74

Solutions 75

Index 101

Table of Figures

FIGURE 1 Interdependencies between Create WBS, Define Activities, and Sequence Activities 5

FIGURE 2 WBS Work Packages, Activities and Tasks 7

FIGURE 3 Schedule-related attributes of an activity 9

FIGURE 4 Predecessor and successor activities 16

FIGURE 5 Finish-Start (FS) Sequence: Activity A must finish before Activity B can start 17

FIGURE 6 Finish-Finish (FF) Sequence: Activity A must finish before Activity B can finish. 18

FIGURE 7 Start-Finish (SF) Sequence: Activity A must start before Activity B can finish 19

FIGURE 8 Start-Start (SS) Sequence: Activity A must start before Activity B can start. 19

FIGURE 9 An Activity-On-Node network diagram with two paths 20

FIGURE 10 Using activity duration to determine Critical Path(s) in AON 26

FIGURE 11 Using activity float to determine Critical Path(s) in AON....................28

What This Guide Is About

During my own study for PMP® certification exam, I had no choice but to consult several books in order to grasp the basics of Precedence Diagramming Method (PDM)/Activity-On-Node (AON) and Critical Path Method (CPM). I found that this topic among many others got limited coverage in many study guides and it was not detailed enough or the definitions left me looking for more explanation. I referred several books in order to study and get a complete understanding of specific topics and one of these topics was what this guide focuses on. At these times, I wished there were topical guides from which I could acquire foundational knowledge and understanding on specific topics, and help me prepare efficiently for the exam. This basic study guide on PDM/AON and CPM aims to meet this need. This guide will provide readers with adequate topical knowledge and hands-on problem solving skills on PDM/AON and CPM for PMP® and CAPM® exams.

I have provided numerous solved examples that the reader can use in order to fully grasp the concepts and techniques. In addition, I have provided solutions with adequate explanations for the practice exercises at the end of this study guide. The reader will be best served to solve the exercises on their own and then compare their own solutions with the solutions provided. All solutions have been provided *step-by-step* with diagrams to allow the reader to understand them visually since project network diagrams are graphic representations.

What this Guide Is <u>Not</u> About

This guide does not aim to cover the entire topic of Project Network Diagrams including its actual construction using any available software. This guide will be limited to the basics of Precedence Diagramming Method (PDM)/Activity-On-Node (AON) and Critical Path Method (CPM). For example, details regarding other network diagram types like Activity-On-Arrow (AOA) are not covered. Since this guide is geared towards readers preparing for PMP®/CAPM® exams and is primarily based on PMBOK®, 4th edition, it may not meet the needs and/or expectations outside of this scope.

Who This Guide Is For

This guide is for anyone who is interested in knowing the basics of Precedence Diagramming Method (PDM)/Activity-On-Node (AON) and Critical Path Method (CPM) especially to prepare for PMP® and CAPM® exams. However, the reader does not have to necessarily be preparing for PMP® or CAPM® certification exams in order to use this guide. The stepwise easy-to-understand style of this guide does not require the reader to have any prior knowledge. Using this guide, the reader will be able to:

- Learn basics related to Precedence Diagramming Method (PDM)/Activity-On-Node (AON) network diagrams and use of Critical Path Method (CPM),
- Obtain all concepts required for the PMP® and CAPM® exams for this topic based on PMBOK®, 4th edition,
- Clear and Concise coverage of all terms related to the topic along with practical examples for better and easier comprehension,
- Hands-on learning using step-by-step Solved Examples with progressively increasing levels of difficulty, and
- Test understanding and knowledge with practice exercises at the end, and compare solutions with included step-by-step detailed solutions.

Feedback

Every work and every effort has room for improvement and in the spirit of continuous improvement, I definitely request and encourage readers to submit *constructive* feedback regarding this guide. Your constructive feedback will immensely assist me in further improving and enhancing the value of this guide for future readers. I will not be able to respond to individual reader questions or feedback but please be assured that I will definitely read them and distill valuable suggestions from them. If any reader's feedback is used in this guide, I will acknowledge the reader's contribution in the guide's Acknowledgement section in a future edition. So, please include your name and profession or professional title along with your feedback.

Section 1: Get the Basics

"Your summer project has only one activity—Play Video Games!"

Summary

Development of Project Network Diagrams is an important part of Activity Sequencing in Schedule Management of a project. There are different types of network schedule but this guide will focus on those that are created using Precedence Diagramming Method (PDM) which is also known as Activity-On-Node (AON[1]). We will not cover Arrow Diagramming Method (ADM) also known as Activity-on-Arrow (AOA[2]) as this is not commonly used nowadays. In addition, we will see how to use the Critical Path Method (CPM) technique to analyze activity network diagrams to determine several important schedule-related aspects for the project and its activities—activities that cannot be delayed and those that can be delayed, minimum project start-to-finish time and early start and finish times along with late start and finish times.

Introduction

In retrospect, I must admit that I had scant knowledge about project management when I started my career as an IT professional. At that time, it was mostly about tasks that got assigned that had to get done within an expected timeframe. However, with the passage of time, and with increasing experience and exposure, I gained understanding and insight into the bigger world of projects and project management moving beyond the initial limits of assigned task boundaries. My own keen observation and curiosity helped me understand many facets of project management through professional experience. Needless to say that I did not find this adequate as practice standards differed from organization to organization and sometimes within the same organization. In addition, the complexity of processes and workflows differed or processes and/or workflows didn't exist at all. Through the maze of different practices, procedures and differing organizational standards, I tried to understand why certain projects were successful and certain projects were not successful. As my interest grew in this area, I found myself drawn towards the practice and knowledge of project management.

---

[1] PDM or AON has also been referred to as "*task-on-the-node (TON) method*" (pp. 164, Wysocki, 2009)
[2] ADM or AOA has also been referred to as "*task-on-the-arrow (TOA) method*" (pp.163, Wysocki, 2009)

Project Management Institute's (PMI®) PMBOK®[3] has a wealth of concepts and knowledge related to project management that I feel every IT professional must be familiar with even if he or she is not directly involved in project management. The reason is that project's are done by teams and if each team member understands the concepts, processes, stages and other details related to projects, it will be immensely easier to work in cohesion with awareness as to why things are being done a certain way and even intervene to suggest/undertake preventive or corrective measures if threats are discerned in the project and might have escaped the project management team's attention and diligence.

Enough said about the importance of increasing one's knowledge regarding project management, the task is by no means small. During my preparation for the PMP® exam, in addition to studying the PMBOK®, I had to study several PMP® exam guide books. While PMBOK® does an excellent job of covering the concepts, the "how" part is not really there. In my own study I wanted to learn not just the "what" but also the "how" as I always strongly believed that knowledge is best served when it is used and when it is applied it can even serve to enhance knowledge itself. I found several topics that required lot of time and extensive research using different sources in order to comprehend them sometimes both on the "what" as well as the "how". It is from this personal experience that I realized it would be useful to bring it all together, topic-by-topic, so that an interested reader can easily study the basic essentials and to get a foundation and at the same time be well prepared for the PMP® exam. The value in preparing for the PMP® exam, in my opinion, lies in acquiring and testing one's knowledge of all the knowledge areas as defined in PMI®'s PMBOK®.

The three most important constraints that a Project Manager must handle for any project are: Schedule, Cost and Scope. These three constraints make up the Project Management Triangle also known as *Triple Constraint*. Project Time Management which is an important part of Project Management is done to handle a project's schedule constraint. In this guide, we will focus on the topic of Precedence Diagramming Method (PDM)/Activity-On-Node (AON) network diagrams within the knowledge area

---

[3] PMBOK® is PMI®'s *A Guide to the Project Management Body of Knowledge*. The most recent edition is the 4th edition published in 2008.

of Project Time Management in order to gain basic understanding of this specific type of network diagram which is currently more popular than another type of network diagram called Arrow Diagramming Method (ADM). *PDM is also known as Activity-On-Node or AON.* Next we will get an understanding of a specific technique called Critical Path Method (CPM) which is used for analyzing AONs to determine project schedule details and is a very valuable technique to know both from a conceptual as well as application point-of-view.

In this guide we start first with understanding what an activity is and then we look at network diagrams like PDM or AON that include activities. It is important to understand that the two knowledge areas Project Scope Management and Project Time Management are related to each other. *Create WBS* in Project Scope Management creates Work Breakdown Structure (WBS) which has the smallest decomposed work units called work packages. The work packages from the WBS along with the WBS Dictionary are used to define activities in the *Define Activities* process in Project Time Management. Outputs from Define Activities process such as Activity List and Activity Attributes are used in the *Sequence Activities* process whose outputs include Project Network Diagram(s). These interdependencies are shown in Figure 1.

FIGURE 1 Interdependencies between Create WBS, Define Activities, and Sequence Activities

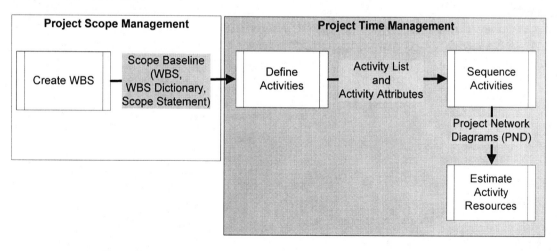

Based on these interdependencies, we first look in detail at the relationship between WBS work packages, activities, and tasks, and then in detail at what

an activity is followed by how activities are used in PDM network diagrams. In this guide we will cover the following:

- Basics of an Activity's schedule-related attributes: Early Start (ES), Early Finish (EF), Late Start (LS), Late Finish (LF), Float/Slack, and Duration.
- Discussion on Lag Time, Lead Time, and different types of activity Float.
- Basics of Precedence Diagramming Method (PDM)/Activity-On-Node (AON) network diagrams.
- Activity Sequence Dependency: Finish-Start (FS), Start-Start (SS), Finish-Finish (FF), and Start-Finish (SF).
- Critical Path, Critical Activities, and Hypercritical Activities
- Forward Pass and Backward Pass methods for computing Early Start (ES), Early Finish (EF), Late Start (LS), and Late Finish (LF).
- Solved examples using Forward Pass and Backward Pass.

Understanding Basics of an Activity: Building Block of Activity-On-Node (AON)

It is important to understand what an activity is and also what a task is in the context of project management. Activities are defined based on work package elements which are the lowest level elements of a project's Work Breakdown Structure (WBS)[4]. This means that a work package element can have one or more activities. Each activity in turn can have one or more tasks. When an activity has only one task, the terms can be used interchangeably—task for activity or vice versa.

---

[4] Work Breakdown Structures (WBS) are created as part of Project Scope Management as per PMBOK®, 4th Edition, and will not be discussed in this guide.

FIGURE 2 WBS Work Packages, Activities and Tasks

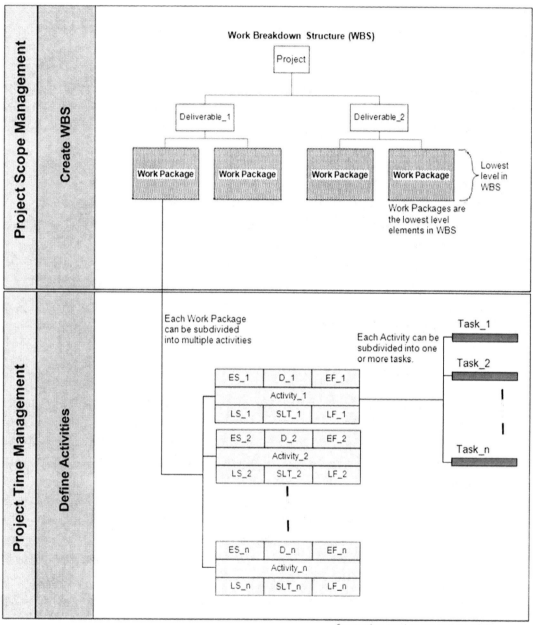

In all our discussions in this guide we will assume that an activity always has only one task. An activity will require inputs and will have fixed time from start to finish and after it finishes it has an output which can be an input for one or more dependent activities or may be an end output as in a deliverable.

Each activity has a defined start date (or time) and an end date (or time) along with duration. At this point, it is important to understand two terms—duration and effort—in order to ensure there is no misconception about each of them.

Duration: This is the *actual* time required to complete an activity. Actual time is determined by taking into consideration the actual time worked based on number of assigned resources and not considering non-working time (e.g. holidays, weekends, resource vacations or unavailability and any other factor.) This is the interval time period between an activity's actual start and end time periods. Duration is also called *Span time*[5] (Portny, 2010). It can be determined as follows:

Duration = (EF – ES) + 1

Or

Duration = (LF – LS) + 1

Effort: This is the estimated number of person-hours[6] that will be required to complete an activity where person-hours is the total amount of work that can be done by a person in one hour. Note that, the time period can be expressed in different units of measure for time e.g. days, weeks, years, and so on such as person-years.

Example: The landscaping for a mansion takes 5 full business days employing 4 employees. Then the duration for this work is 5 full business days. This means that if work begins on Thursday, then it ends on Wednesday where the weekend—Saturday and Sunday—is considered non-working days and this is not considered as part of the

---

[5] According to Newell (2002), Span is the time interval between the start and finish times of an activity, and that it is not same as duration. For our discussions, we will not include further discussion on this, and use the duration concept for activities.

[6] Also previously referred to as man-hours.

actual duration. The effort for this work will be 20 person-days which means that it would take one person 20 full business days to complete the work if he/she were to do it alone.

Duration (or Span time) and Effort can be defined as a unit of time e.g. days, weeks, months, and so on. Duration and Effort of an activity can be fixed or can change depending on factors such as assigned resources.

FIGURE 3 Schedule-related attributes of an activity

Early Start (ES)	Duration	Early Finish (EF)
Activity Name		
Late Start (LS)	Slack	Late Finish (LF)

Each activity in an AON has two types of Start Times and two types of Finish Times. The two types of start times an Activity has are as follows:

(a) *Early Start (ES):* This is the earliest time an activity can be started since the start of the project regardless of whether it is the very first activity or a later activity. It is denoted as ES and diagrammatically placed at the top left corner of an activity represented as a rectangle or square in an AON. For the first activity in a project network diagram, ES is set to 1 regardless of the unit of measure used for time e.g. hours, days, weeks, etc.

(b) *Late Start (LS):* This is the latest time an activity can be started since the start of the project regardless of whether it is the very first activity or a later activity. If the activity is started later than LS, then the delay can impact the project's completion date unless certain mitigation steps are taken. It is denoted as LS and diagrammatically placed at the bottom left corner of an activity represented as a rectangle or square in an AON.

The two types of finish times an Activity has are as follows:

(a) *Early Finish (EF):* This is the earliest time an activity can be completed since the start of the project. Determination of an activity's EF depends on the activity's ES and duration It is denoted as EF and diagrammatically placed at the top right corner of an activity represented as a rectangle or square in an AON.

(b) **Late Finish (LF):** This is the latest time an activity can be completed since the start of the project. If the activity does not finish by this time then the project completion date will be affected. It is denoted as LF and diagrammatically placed at the bottom right corner of an activity represented as a rectangle or square in an AON.

Float: Float is defined as the total time an activity can be delayed without adversely impacting the start of any of its successor activities or the project scheduled completion time. Each activity in a network diagram has its own float. Activity float can be derived based on the activity's ES, EF, LS and LF. Float can also be referred to as *Slack*. Float or Slack can be of several different types:

(a) **Free Float**: This is the amount of time an activity can be allowed to take longer than its actual duration without impacting the Early Start (ES) of any of its successor activities. It is also known as *Secondary Float*. It can be determined as follows:
Free Float of predecessor activity = Early Start of successor activity *minus* Early Finish of predecessor activity.
Alternatively, *Free Float of predecessor activity* = (Early Start of successor activity *minus* Early Start of predecessor activity) *minus* Duration of predecessor activity *plus* one.

Note:

- ♦ Free Float is calculated using Early Start (ES) of successor activity and Early Finish (EF) of predecessor activity but <u>not</u> using Late Start (LS) and Late Finish (LF) for successor and predecessor activities respectively.
- ♦ *Free Float can never be negative.*

Example

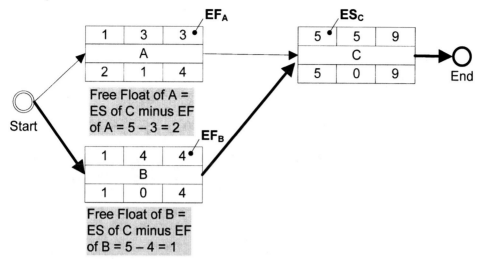

Free Float of A = ES of C minus EF of A = 5 – 3 = 2

Free Float of B = ES of C minus EF of B = 5 – 4 = 1

(b) **Start Float**: This is the difference between LS and ES of an activity. *Start Float* = Late Start (LS) *minus* Early Start (ES). This allows us to determine the time period by which the start of an activity can be delayed without impacting project completion date.

Example

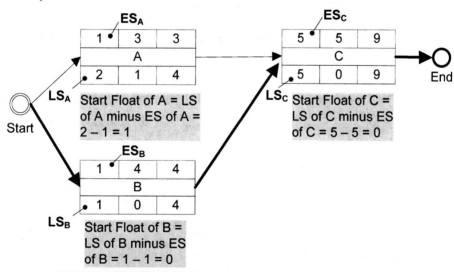

Start Float of A = LS of A minus ES of A = 2 – 1 = 1

Start Float of C = LS of C minus ES of C = 5 – 5 = 0

Start Float of B = LS of B minus ES of B = 1 – 1 = 0

Note:
Since Start Float of B = Start Float of C = 0 means that the start of these activities cannot be delayed without delaying the project's completion. Therefore, the path *Start-B-C-End* is a **Critical Path**.

(c) **Finish Float**: This is the difference between LF and EF of an activity. *Finish Float* = Late Finish (LF) *minus* Early Finish (EF). This allows us to determine the time period by which the completion of an activity can be delayed without impacting project completion date.

Example

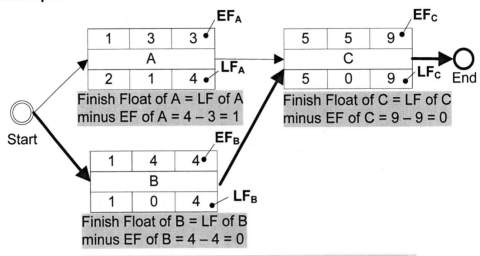

Finish Float of A = LF of A minus EF of A = 4 – 3 = 1

Finish Float of C = LF of C minus EF of C = 9 – 9 = 0

Finish Float of B = LF of B minus EF of B = 4 – 4 = 0

Note:
Since Finish Float of B = Finish Float of C = 0 means that the completion of these activities cannot be delayed without delaying the project's completion. Therefore, the path *Start-B-C-End* is a **Critical Path**.

(d) **Total Float**: Total Float, also known as *Float* or *Positive Float*, is the total time an activity can be delayed from its early start without impacting the project's completion date. It can be determined by using one of the following three methods:

> **Method 1**: *Total Float* = Late Start (LS) *minus* Early Start (ES)

> **Method 2**: *Total Float* = Late Finish (LF) *minus* Early Finish (EF)

> **Method 3**: *Total Float* = Late Finish (LF) *minus* Early Start (ES) *minus* Duration *plus* one

---

Note:

Based on the above formulas for Method 1 and Method 2, it can be stated that *Total Float = Start Float* or *Total Float = Finish Float*.

Example

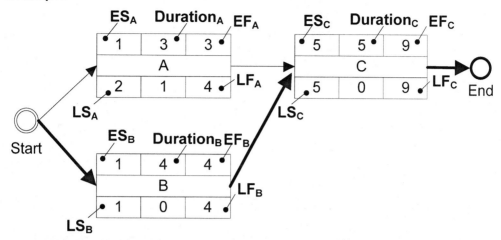

Note:
Since Total Float of B = Total Float of C = 0 means that these activities cannot be delayed without delaying the project's completion. Therefore, the path *Start-B-C-End* is a **Critical Path**.

Activity	Calculation Method	Calculation
A	Total Float (TF) = Start Float of A	$TF_A = LS_A - ES_A = 2 - 1 = 1$
	Total Float (TF) = Finish Float of A	$TF_A = LF_A - EF_A = 4 - 3 = 1$
	Total Float (TF) = Late Finish of A *minus* Early Start of A *minus* Duration of A *plus* one	$TF_A = LF_A - ES_A - Duration_A + 1 = 4 - 1 - 3 + 1 = 1$
B	Total Float (TF) = Start Float of B	$TF_B = LS_B - ES_B = 1 - 1 = 0$
	Total Float (TF) = Finish Float of B	$TF_B = LF_B - EF_B = 4 - 4 = 0$
	Total Float (TF) = Late Finish of B *minus* Early Start of B *minus* Duration of B *plus* one	$TF_B = LF_B - ES_B - Duration_B + 1 = 4 - 1 - 4 + 1 = 0$
C	Total Float (TF) = Start Float of C	$TF_C = LS_C - ES_C = 9 - 9 = 0$
	Total Float (TF) = Finish Float of C	$TF_C = LF_C - EF_C = 5 - 5 = 0$
	Total Float (TF) = Late Finish of C *minus* Early Start of C *minus* Duration of C *plus* one	$TF_C = LF_C - ES_C - Duration_C + 1 = 9 - 5 - 5 + 1 = 0$

(e) **Project Float**: This is the total time the project can be delayed without adversely affecting the project's completion date as per customer expectations. In other words, *Project Float* = Project's Customer Expected Completion Duration *minus* Project's Critical Path[7] duration.

Note:

> It is possible for Project Float to be negative if the project's expected completion duration based on the customer's completion date for the project is sooner than the project's planned completion date. In such cases, schedule compression techniques will have to be used.

(f) **Negative Float**: Negative Float for an activity occurs when the difference between LS and ES or LF and EF is negative. In other words, negative float occurs when Late Start (LS) is earlier than Early Start (ES) or Late Finish (LF) is earlier than Early Finish (EF).

For an activity, when LS – ES < 0 it implies that LS < ES (Late Start is less than Early Start), and also, when LF – EF < 0 it implies that LF < EF (Late Finish is less than Early Finish.)

Note:

> Negative Float can occur when one or more of the following situations take place:
> - The planned duration of an activity network diagram path is greater than the actual available time.
> - When critical activities or critical path is delayed or extended.
> - When the planned schedule is longer than the actual available time.

In order to remedy negative float occurrences, it might be necessary to undertake schedule compression techniques in order to adjust the planned schedule within the expected time frame or under certain circumstances negotiate with the customer to change the expected completion date for the project.

---

[7] Critical Path will be defined and discussed in subsequent sections.

(g) **Negative Total Float**: This is the time by which the duration of an activity or an entire path has to be reduced in order to meet a pre-determined project completion date.

Differences between Free Float and Total Float:

1. Free Float relates to an activity's slack time so as not to impact its successor activity's early start time, while Total Float is related to an activity's slack time so as not to impact the project's completion date.
2. Free Float for an activity exists *only* if it has at least one successor activity, while Total Float exists for any and all activities even if an activity does not have any successor activity.
3. Free Float of an activity can be less than or equal to Total Float of the activity but cannot be greater than Total Float (Wysocki, 2009).

Understanding Basics of Precedence Diagramming Method (PDM)/Activity-On-Node (AON) Diagram

Precedence Diagramming Method (PDM) is a commonly used project network diagram. The other method that is not used as often is Arrow Diagramming Method (ADM). PDM is also known as Activity-On-Node (AON) and ADM is also known as Activity-on-Arrow (AOA). ADM and AOA will not be discussed as the focus will be on PDM/AON which the PMBOK® 4th edition covers.

PDM uses sequence relationship between activities in the network diagram. There are four relationships that PDM uses in establishing sequence between activities and the type of relationship used will depend on the nature of dependency between two activities. The four relationship types are—(a) Finish-Start (FS), (b) Finish-Finish (FF), (c) Start-Start (SS), and (d) Start-Finish (SF). These relationship types are defined in detail in this section. In addition to the relationship types, lead and/or lag can be specified if a dependent or successor activity can have a head start or delay in its start.

An AON network diagram has nodes which are connected by arrows. Each node is an activity. The arrow linking one node to another show the sequence in which the activities should occur. In other words, the arrows denote the dependency between activities. The first activity or activities in a network diagram occur after the Start event, and thus have no predecessor activities and can have one or more successor activities. The last activity or activities will have no successors and can have one or more predecessor activities. Intermediate activities will have both predecessor and successor activities.

FIGURE 4 Predecessor and successor activities

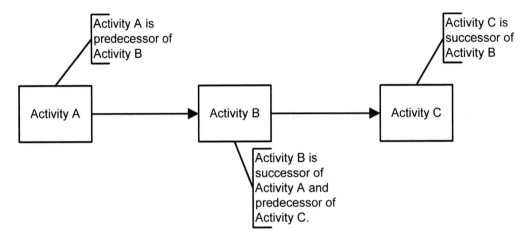

Besides identifying an activity's position in the network diagram, activity sequencing also assists in determining the sequence dependency between activities. For any two activities in a project network diagram, there is one activity, commonly referred to as a predecessor activity, at the tail of the sequence-relationship arrow and the other activity, commonly referred to as the successor activity, is at the head of the sequence-relationship arrow.

There are four types of sequence-based relationship dependencies[8] that can exist between any two activities. A project network diagram may not include all the four dependencies. Each relationship can be defined as follows: *Predecessor activity has to <first word of the relationship> before its successor activity can <second word of the relationship>*. The four activity relationship dependencies are described below:

(a) **Finish-Start** (FS): Predecessor activity has to *finish* before its successor activity can *start*. It is denoted as FS but since this is the most common

---

[8] Dependency between tasks can also be based on the nature of relationship between them. PMBOK®, 4th Edition, identifies dependency types— Mandatory, Discretionary and External. For detailed discussion on each of these dependency types, please refer to Project Time Management, PMBOK® 4th Edition.

occurring relationship between activities, the relationship arrow is not labeled as FS when this relationship exists between two activities. It is also referred to as Finish-to-Start.

Note:

♦ In this dependency, constraint is on the completion of predecessor activity and start of successor activity and there is no constraint as to when the predecessor starts or when the successor finishes.
♦ The successor activity can start anytime but not before the completion of its predecessor activity. Therefore, successor activity is not required to start at the same time its predecessor activity finishes.

FIGURE 5 Finish-Start (FS) Sequence: Activity A must finish before Activity B can start

Finish-to-Start (FS):

Example 1: Students must officially register for classes before they can attend classes.

Example 2: Students must have completed required pre-requisite courses before they can register for graduate-level courses.

(b) **Finish-Finish** *(FF)*: Predecessor activity has to *finish* before its successor activity can *finish*. It is denoted by FF. It is also referred to as Finish-to-Finish.

Note:

♦ In this dependency, constraint is on the completion of predecessor activity and completion of successor activity and

---

there is no constraint as to when the predecessor activity or the successor activity starts.

- ♦ The successor activity can finish anytime but not before the predecessor activity finishes. Therefore, successor activity is not required to finish at the same time its predecessor activity finishes.

FIGURE 6 Finish-Finish (FF) Sequence: Activity A must finish before Activity B can finish.

Finish-to-Finish (FF):

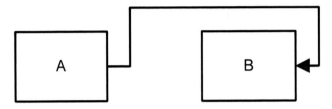

Example 1: The illustrator must finish the illustrations before manuscript can be finalized.

Example 2: As part of a local car showroom's extensive renovations, painting of interior walls must finish before art displays on walls can be finished.

(c) **Start-Finish** *(SF)*: This dependency is not very common. In this dependency, predecessor activity has to *start* before its successor activity can *finish*. It is denoted by SF. It is also referred to as Start-to-Finish.

Note:

- ♦ In this dependency, constraint is on the start of predecessor activity and completion of successor activity and there is no constraint as to when the predecessor activity can finish or the successor activity can start.
- ♦ The successor activity can finish anytime but not before the predecessor activity starts. Therefore, successor activity is not required to finish at the same time its predecessor activity starts.

FIGURE 7 Start-Finish (SF) Sequence: Activity A must start before Activity B can finish

Start-to-Finish (SF):

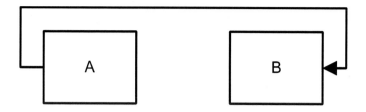

Example 1: In order to bake the wedding cake, the cook starts preheating the oven before he finishes preparing the cake's batter.
Example 2: The gardener must start selecting the flower plants before preparation of flower beds are finished.

(d) **Start-Start** *(SS)*: In this dependency, predecessor activity has to *start* before its successor activity can *start*. It is also referred to as Start-to-Start.

Note:

♦ In this dependency, the constraint is on the start of predecessor and successor activities and there is no constraint as to when the predecessor activity or the successor activity finishes.
♦ The successor activity can start anytime but not before the predecessor activity starts. Therefore, successor activity is not required to start at the same time its predecessor activity starts.

FIGURE 8 Start-Start (SS) Sequence: Activity A must start before Activity B can start.

Start-to-Start (SS):

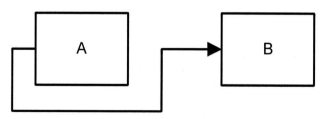

Example 1: A certain political party must start fund collection before it can start its election campaign. Fund collection can be completed at any time even after the election campaign has started.

Example 2: A charitable organization must start collecting donations before the annual charity festival can start. The organization can continue its collection of donations even after the charity festival starts.

A specific sequence of activities from the Start event of the network diagram to the End event is known as *Path* and a network diagram can have one or more paths. One or more activities can be common between different paths in a network diagram.

FIGURE 9 An Activity-On-Node network diagram with two paths

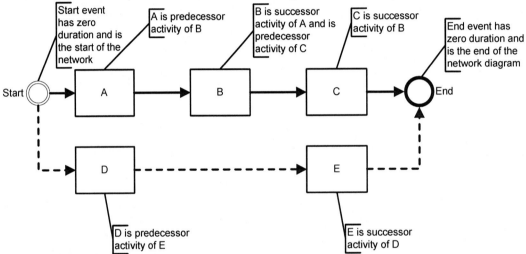

Figure 9 shows the network diagram shown above is an Activity-On-Node diagram and it has the following features:

1. Start and End events have zero duration.

2. Each activity is represented by a rectangle and is called a Node. Instead of a box or rectangle, it can be represented by a circle. We will use rectangle to represent activity throughout this guide.

3. Each activity is connected by arrow depicting the relationship and sequence between the activities.

4. There are 5 activities—A, B, C, D, and E.

5. The logical relationship between predecessor and successor activity for the activities is Finish-Start (FS). Since it is FS, the relationship arrows are not labeled as FS.

6. There are two paths:
    (a) Start-A-B-C-End (shown with solid arrows)
    (b) Start-D-E-End (shown with dashed arrows)

TABLE 1 Table shows a non-graphical representation of the Network Diagram shown in Figure 9

Predecessor	Successor
Start	A, D
A	B
B	C
D	E
C, E	End

Now that we have discussed the different types of possible dependencies between activities, we will look at how these dependencies can be further qualified to cover cases when successor's scheduled start can have a head start or can be delayed using Lead Time or Lag Time respectively.

(a) **Lag**: The time one or more successor activities can be delayed before it can start after its predecessor(s) actually complete(s) is called Lag Time. Lag is *positive time* added to an activity so that its early start is delayed by the specified lag time.

Example:

A bank customer's loan application will require 5 days before an official decision is mailed out. This means that after the activity of loan application submission finishes the dependent or successor activity—mail loan decision—will start earliest only after 5 days. Therefore, an additional 5 days get added to the successor activity's early start date.

Finish-Start (FS) with Lag time:

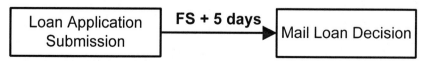

(b)**Lead**: The time one or more successor activities can be started prior to the completion of its predecessor activity is known as Lead. Lead is *negative time* for an activity in order to allow its early start to occur ahead of schedule.

Example:

In making a pasta dish, the recipe has two activities—prepare the sauce and boil the pasta--and preparing the sauce must finish before boiling the pasta can start. Therefore, preparing the sauce is the preceding activity and boiling the pasta is the successor activity, and the dependency between the activities is Finish-to-Start (FS). However, the cook determines that instead of waiting for preceding activity--prepare the sauce--to finish, the successor activity--boiling the pasta--can be started 30 minutes earlier than its earliest start time. In this case, the Finish-to-Start dependency has a lead time of 30 minutes.

Finish-Start (FS) with Lead Time:

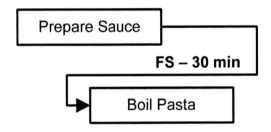

In the next section we will cover all the basics related to Critical Path Method (CPM).

Section 2: Critical Path Method

"I thought I was very clear—you have NO Slack Time!"

In this section, we will cover the basics of Critical Path Method technique which is commonly used with Activity-On-Node (AON) networks to determine schedule related attributes for individual activities and for the entire network.

Understanding Critical Activities and Critical Path

A network diagram for a project will have at least one sequence of specific activities from Start event to End event of the diagram and it is called a *Network Path* or simply *Path*. In an activity network diagram, there are one or more paths. The total duration of each path is determined by adding duration of each activity in that path. The path with the highest total duration is called the *critical path* and each activity in this path is known as *critical activity*. Critical activities or activities on the critical path have *no* slack time and thus cannot be delayed without affecting the scheduled completion date for the project. Therefore, a critical activity will have the following characteristics:

- Either Total Float *is equal to* or *is less than* 0
- Either Late Start (LS) *is equal to* or *is less than* Early Start (ES)
- Either Late Finish (LF) *is equal to* or *is less than* Early Finish (EF)

Since activities on a critical path have no available float or slack, any delay or duration extension to even one of the critical activities can adversely impact the project's planned completion date. A project network diagram can have one or more critical paths. *Duration of the project is the total duration of the longest path in the network diagram* and this is also the network's critical path. A network diagram can have multiple critical paths when there are multiple paths whose duration is the highest total duration among all paths in the network.

Those paths whose total duration is the next lower in value than the highest total duration are called *Near-Critical Paths* and activities on those paths are called *Near-Critical Activities*.

Hypercritical activities are activities on the critical path which have negative float. These activities require immediate attention as their planned duration exceeds the allotted time frame.

Supercritical activities are activities with negative float and *may not be on a critical path*.

Determine Critical Path in a Project Network Diagram

In order to determine a project network diagram's critical path, it is required to have duration for each activity in the network diagram. There are *two* ways to determine critical path(s) in a project's network diagram.

First Approach: This approach is based on determining path(s) with highest total duration(s). Use the following steps to determine the network diagram's critical path:

Step 1: Identify and list all paths in the project network diagram.

Step 2: For each path identified in Step 1, determine the path's total duration by adding duration of each activity in the path.

Step 3: Compare total durations of the paths, determined in Step 2, and identify path(s) with the highest total duration.

Step 4: Path(s) with highest total duration(s), determined in Step 3, is (are) the Critical Path(s) for the network diagram.

FIGURE 10 Using activity duration to determine Critical Path(s) in AON

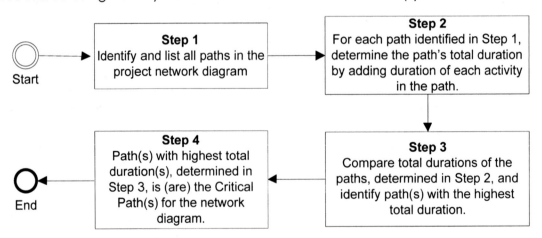

Example: For the project network diagram shown, we will use the total path duration approach to determine its critical path.

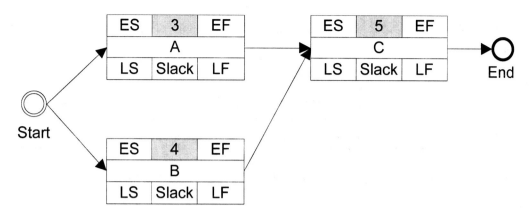

There are two paths in the network diagram:

    1. Start-A-C-End
    2. Start-B-C-End

The duration of Start and End events in a project network diagram is always zero.

The total duration of path Start-A-C-End = T_{AC} = Duration of A + Duration of C = $3 + 5 = 8$

The total duration of path Start-B-C-End = T_{BC} = Duration of B + Duration of C = $4 + 5 = 9$

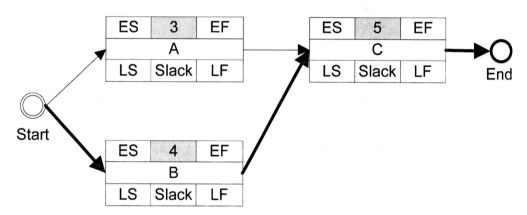

Since $T_{BC} > T_{AC}$, the critical path is *Start-B-C-End* (shown with bold arrows in the diagram above).

Second Approach: This approach is based on determining the float of each activity based on difference between early time periods (start or finish) and late time periods (start or finish). If the activity's float is less than or equal to zero, then that activity is in the critical path. Identifying all such activities between Start and End events of the network diagram helps in identifying the critical path(s).

Note:

This approach uses an activity's EF and ES or LF and LS determined using Forward Pass and Backward Pass respectively, and these techniques are covered in detail in later sections.

Use the steps described below to determine a project network diagram's critical path:

Step 1: Determine ES and EF of each activity in the network diagram using Forward Pass.

Step 2: Determine LS and LF of each activity in the network diagram using Backward Pass.

Step 3: Determine Float of each activity by taking the difference between LS and ES or LF and EF.

Step 4: Identify all activities with float less than or equal to 0. Path(s) in which all activities have float less than or equal to zero in the network diagram, will be the critical path(s).

FIGURE 11 Using activity float to determine Critical Path(s) in AON

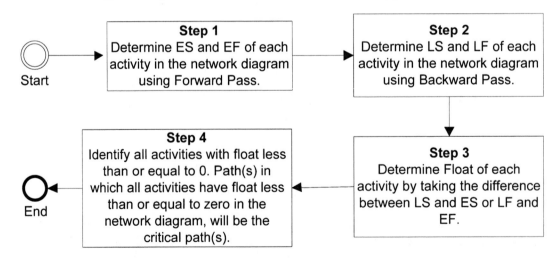

The second approach using activity float is commonly used for large-scale projects, in which using the first approach may not be practical.

Example: For the project network diagram in this example, we will use each activity's float to determine critical path(s). Although this is the same network diagram used in the previous example, each activity's ES, EF, LS, and LF have been calculated using Forward Pass and Backward Pass. The same network diagram has been used intentionally to show that both the approaches yield the same result, i.e. determine the same critical path.

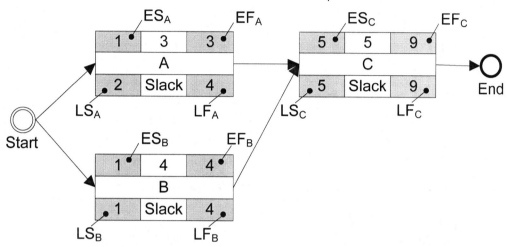

Float for activity A = F_A = $LS_A − ES_A$ = 2 − 1 = 1

Float for activity B = F_B = $LS_B − ES_B$ = 1 − 1 = 0

Float for activity C = F_C = $LS_C − ES_C$ = 5 − 5 = 0

Since, $F_A \neq 0$, then activity A is not a critical activity.

Since $F_B = 0$ and $F_C = 0$, then both F_B and F_C are critical activities.

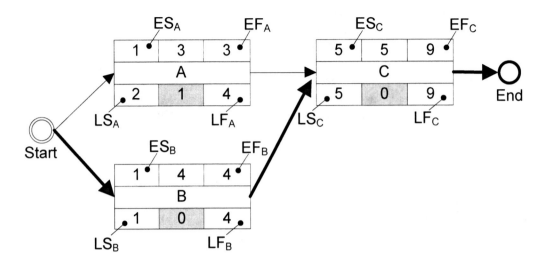

The path *Start-B-C-End* is a critical path, shown with bold arrows in the diagram above, as both activities B and C are critical activities.

Note:

- ♦ A project network diagram can have one or more critical paths and near-critical paths.
- ♦ Project Duration = Project Network Diagram's Critical Path duration.

Section 3: Critical Path Analysis of AON using CPM

"Smoking will not improve your Backward Pass!
Practice will!"

Critical Path Method (CPM) is an important technique that is used on an Activity-On-Node network diagram to determine important schedule related attributes for each activity, the total estimated duration for each path and the total duration for the project. In this guide all discussions regarding the use of CPM on an AON, Finish-to-Start (FS) dependency will be used and the duration of each activity will be provided.

First, we will start with the Forward Pass technique in order to determine the early start and early finish dates for each activity in the network diagram. Second, we will use the Backward Pass technique to determine late start and late finish times for each of the network activities. Third, we will determine the network's critical path(s) and use that to determine total float time for each activity. We will use examples to cover different types of network diagrams in order to get a good understanding of the techniques.

Determining Activity Early Start and Early Finish: Forward Pass

We have already covered the definitions for an activity's Early Start and Early Finish. In this section, we will cover how to determine an activity's Early Start (ES) and Early Finish (EF) using the "forward pass" method.
For a network diagram with *n* number of activities, we can determine ES and EF based on the activity's position in the network diagram as follows:

(a) For 1st activity, the first activity immediately after Start event, $ES_1 = 1$ and $EF_1 = ES_1 +$ duration of 1st activity $- 1$

(b) For m^{th} activity, where $m < n$ and thus an intermediate activity, $ES_m = EF_{m-1} + 1$, where EF_{m-1} is EF of predecessor activity of mth activity, and $EF_m = ES_m +$ duration of mth activity $- 1$

(c) For n^{th} activity, where it is the last activity in the network diagram, $ES_n = EF_{n-1} + 1$, where EF_{n-1} is EF of predecessor activity of nth activity, and $EF_n = ES_n +$ duration of nth activity $- 1$

Example:
We will use a simple network diagram, as shown below, with two activities—A and B—and FS relationship between them. It is given that the duration of activity A is 3 days and Activity B is 2 days.

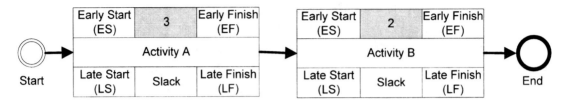

First we will use Forward Pass to determine ES and EF for Activity A and Activity B respectively.

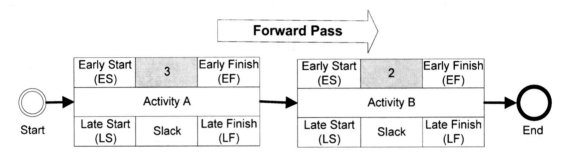

Step 1: Determine ES for Activity A

ES for Activity A is 1 since Activity A is the *first activity* in the network diagram[9].

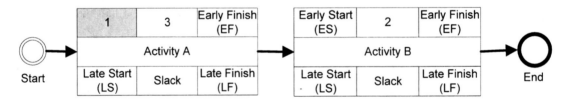

Step 2: Determine EF for Activity A

$EF_A = ES_A + duration_A - 1 = 1 + 3 - 1 = 3$

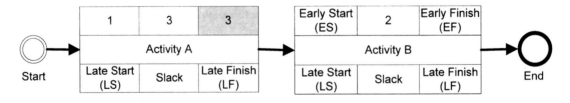

---

[9] There does appear to be another approach of using ES = 0 for the first activity in the network diagram. However, we will not follow this approach. Instead we will use ES = 1 for the first activity in a network diagram.

Step 3: Determine ES for Activity B

$ES_B = EF_A + 1 = 3 + 1 = 4$

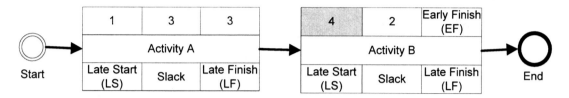

Step 4: Determine EF for Activity B

$EF_B = ES_B + duration_B - 1 = 4 + 2 - 1 = 5$

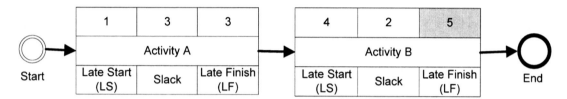

Special Case:

If an activity has more than one predecessor, then the activity's ES = (Highest EF among EFs of the activity's predecessor activities) + 1.

Example: For the portion of the project network diagram shown in this example, the ES and EF for activity C will be determined using Forward Pass. In this special case, activity C has two predecessor activities—A and B.

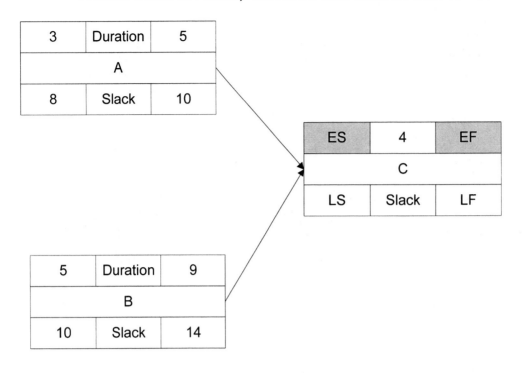

Step 1: Determine ES for activity C

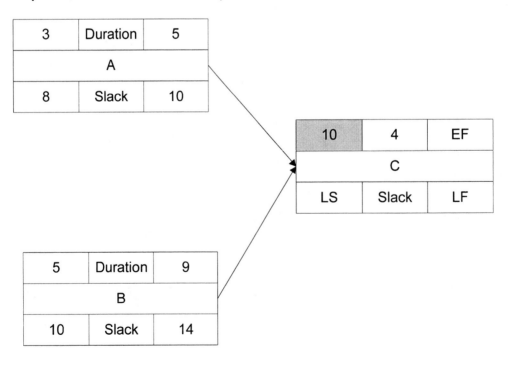

ES_C = (Highest EF among EF of activity A and EF of activity B) + 1

= EF of activity B + 1 = 9 + 1 = 10

Step 2: Determine EF for activity C

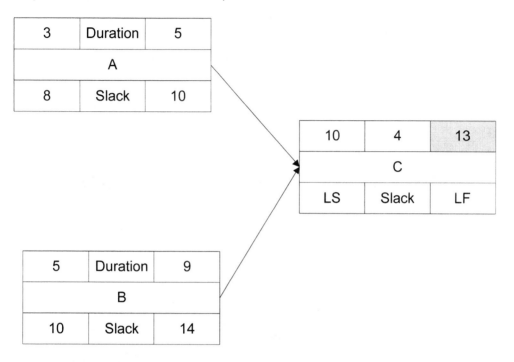

EF_C = ES_C + duration of activity C − 1 = 10 + 4 − 1 = 13

Next we will look at Backward Pass and use the same network diagram to illustrate this technique.

Determining Activity Late Start and Late Finish: Backward Pass

In this section, we will discuss how to determine Late Start and Late Finish for each activity in a network diagram using the "backward pass" method.
For a network diagram with *n* number of activities, we can determine LS and LF using backward pass based on the activity's position in the network diagram as follows:

(a) For n^{th} activity, last as well as the <u>only</u> activity[10] prior to End event in the network diagram, $LF_n = EF_n$ and $LS_n = LF_n$ – duration of nth activity +1.

(b) For m^{th} activity, where m < n and thus an intermediate activity in the network diagram with <u>only</u> one successor activity, $LF_m = LS_{m+1} - 1$, where LS_{m+1} is the Late Start of the successor activity of mth activity, and $LS_m = LF_m$ - duration of mth activity + 1.

(c) For 1st activity, where it is the first activity in the network diagram, $LF_1 = LS_2 - 1$, where LS_2 is the Late Start of its successor activity and only one successor activity, and $LS_1 = LF_1$ - duration of 1st activity + 1.

Example:

Using the same network diagram, we used in the example for Forward Pass, we will use Backward Pass to determine LS and LF for Activity B and Activity A respectively.

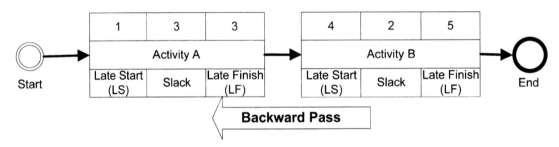

Step 1: Determine LF for Activity B

LF_B for Activity B should be equal to EF_B *since it is the last and only activity in the network.*

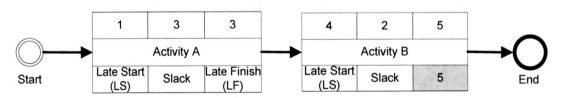

Step 2: Determine LS for Activity B

$LS_B = LF_B$ – $duration_B$ + 1 = 5 – 2 + 1 = 4

---

[10] LF determination for activity with multiple successor activities is covered in the Special Case section.

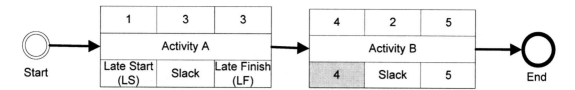

Step 3: Determine LF for Activity A

$LF_A = LS_B - 1 = 4 - 1 = 3$

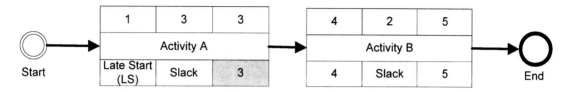

Step 4: Determine LS for Activity A

$LS_A = LF_A - duration_A + 1 = 3 - 3 + 1 = 1$

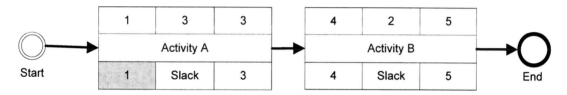

Special Case:

If an activity has more than one successor activity, then the activity's LF = (lowest LS among all LS of the activity's successor activities) – 1

Example: For the portion of the project network diagram shown below, the LS and LF for activity C will be determined using Backward Pass. In this special case, activity C has two successor activities—D and E.

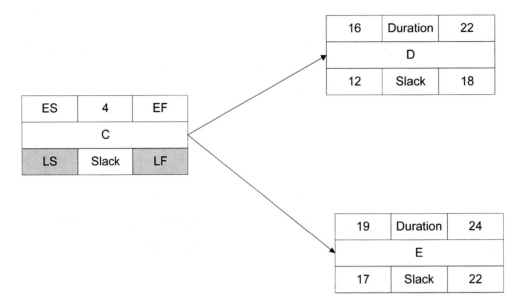

Step 1: Determine LF for activity C

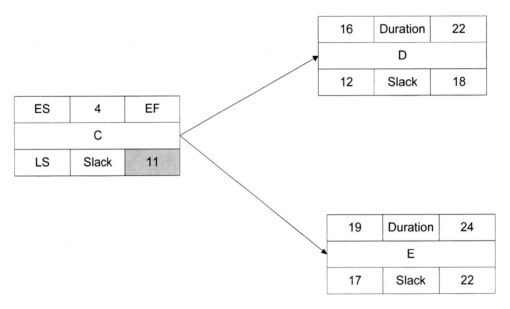

LF_C = (Lowest LS among LS of activity D and LS of activity E) − 1 = 12 − 1 = 11

Step 2: Determine LS of activity C

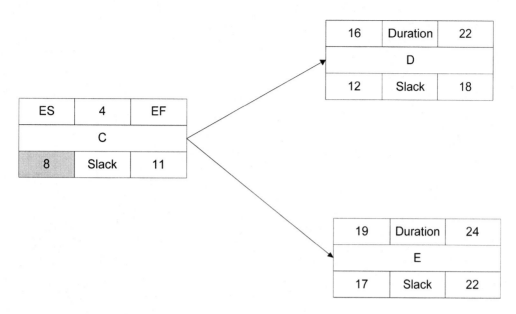

$LS_C = LF_C -$ duration of activity $C + 1 = 11 - 4 + 1 = 8$

Section 4: Solved Examples

"You are better off learning by example."

Example 1

In this example, we will take a simple network diagram with two activities—Activity A and Activity B—to perform Forward Pass and Backward Pass in order to determine ES, EF, LS, and LF. A step-wise walk through the process will provide an understanding of the computation methodology.

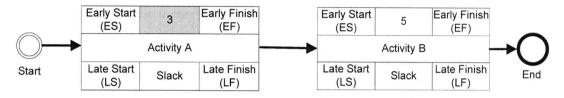

In the network diagram above, Activity A has the duration of 3 days and Activity B has the duration of 5 days.

Let us undertake Forward Pass to determine ES and EF for Activity A and Activity B.

Step 1: Determine ES and EF for Activity A

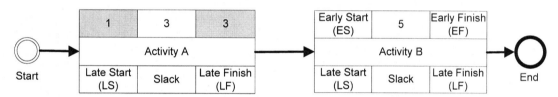

For the first activity in a network diagram, ES is 1.

EF = ES + (duration of Activity A) – 1 = 1 + 3 – 1 = 3

Step 2: Determine ES and EF for activity B

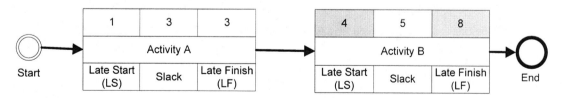

ES for Activity B = EF for Activity A + 1 = 3 + 1 = 4

EF for Activity B = ES for Activity B + duration of Activity B – 1 = 4 + 5 – 1 = 8

In Steps 1 and 2, using Forward Pass, ES and EF for Activity A and Activity B was computed. Now, in Steps 3 and 4, LS and LF for Activity B and Activity A will be determined.

Step 3: Determine LS and LF for Activity B

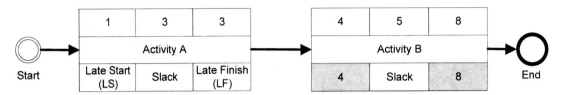

LF for Activity B = EF for Activity B = 8

LS for Activity B = LF for Activity B – duration of Activity B + 1 = 8 – 5 + 1 = 4

Step 4: Determine LS and LF for Activity A

In this final step, we will determine LS and LF for Activity A as explained below.

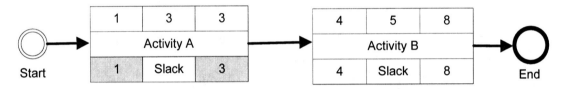

LF for Activity A = LS for Activity B – 1 = 4 – 1 = 3

LS for Activity A = LF for Activity A – duration of activity A + 1 = 3 – 3 + 1 = 1

The Slack for each activity can be determined based on the critical path duration of the network diagram. Since this diagram has only one path, there is only one critical path and its duration is duration of Activity A + duration of activity B which is 3 + 5 = 8 days. Also, it is known that the slack or float time for activities on the critical path i.e. critical activities is 0. Therefore, the Slack for both Activity A and Activity B will be 0.

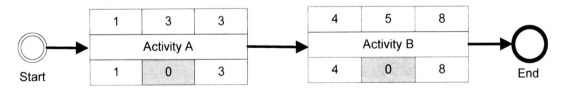

Now that we have covered the basics of Forward Pass and Backward Pass in Example 1, we will cover progressively advanced cases in the other examples. In all the examples, we will use network diagrams with activities mentioned in the table below:

Activity	Duration (days)
Activity A	3
Activity B	5
Activity C	7
Activity D	2
Activity E	9

Note that in the examples 2, 3 and 4, first four activities mentioned in the table above will be used—Activity A, Activity B, Activity C and Activity D. In the last example, Example 5, all five activities mentioned in the table above will be used.

Example 2

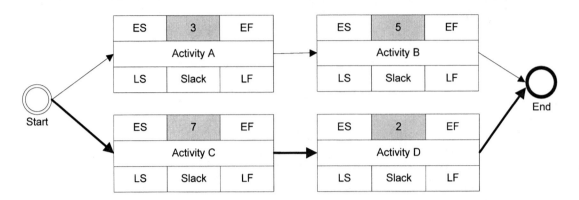

For the network diagram shown above, we will determine all the attributes—ES, EF, LS, LF, and Slack—for each of the activities using their given durations.

Step 1: Determine Critical Path

Duration of path Start-Activity A–Activity B-End = Duration of Activity A *plus* Duration of Activity B = 3 + 5 = 8. *Note that Start and End events always have zero duration.*

Duration of path Start-Activity C–Activity D-End = Duration of Activity C *plus* Duration of Activity D = 7 + 2 = 9

Critical Path is the path with the highest duration which is path *Start-Activity C–Activity D-End*. It is highlighted with bold arrows.

Step 2: Determine ES and EF for Activity A and Activity C

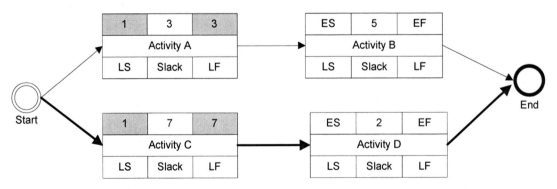

Activity A:

ES = 1

EF = ES + (duration of Activity A) − 1 = 1 + 3 - 1 = 3

Activity C:

ES = 1

EF = ES + (duration of Activity C) − 1 = 1 + 7 − 1 = 7

Step 3: Determine ES and EF for Activity B and Activity D

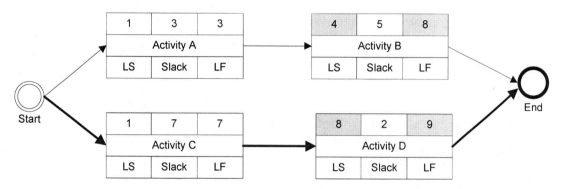

Activity B:

ES = EF of Activity A + 1 = 3 + 1 = 4

EF = ES + (duration of Activity B) − 1 = 4 + 5 − 1 = 8

Activity D:

ES = EF of Activity C + 1 = 7 + 1 = 8

EF = ES + (duration of Activity D) − 1 = 8 + 2 - 1 = 9

Step 4: Determine LS and LF for Activity B and Activity D

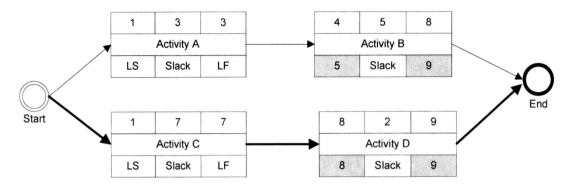

Activity D:

LF = EF of last activity in the critical path = EF of Activity D = 9

LS = LF – (duration of Activity D) + 1 = 9 – 2 + 1 = 8

Activity B:

LF = LF of last activity in the critical path = LF of Activity D = 9

LS = LF – (duration of Activity B) + 1 = 9 – 5 + 1 = 5

Step 5: Determine LS and LF for Activity A and Activity C

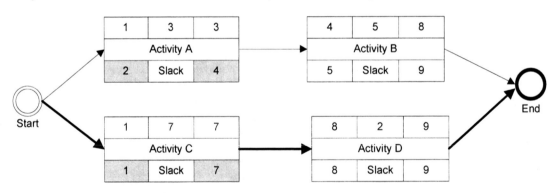

Activity A:

LF = LS of Activity B – 1 = 5 – 1 = 4

LS = LF – (duration of Activity A) + 1 = 4 – 3 + 1 = 2

Activity C:

LF = LS of Activity D – 1 = 8 – 1 = 7

LS = LF – (duration of Activity C) + 1 = 7 – 7 + 1 = 1

Step 6: Determine Activity Slack

Now, we have to determine Slack for the activities in the network diagram.

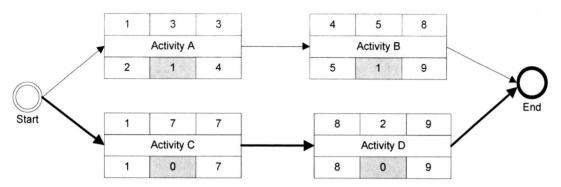

Critical Path is the path with the highest duration which is path *Start-Activity C–Activity D-End*.

Slack for activities in path Start-Activity A–Activity B-End = Critical Path Duration *minus* Duration of path Start-Activity A–Activity B-End = 9 – 8 = 1[11]

Slack for activities in path Start-Activity C–Activity D-End = 0 as they are on the critical path.

---

[11] Slack can also be computed by determining the difference between Late Start (LS) and Early Start (ES) or Late Finish (LF) and Early Finish (EF).

Example 3

In this example, we will look at two specific aspects—(1) determining LF when network diagram has multiple terminal activities, and (2) determining LF for an activity when it has multiple successor activities. The Critical Path is *Start-Activity A-Activity C-End* and it is highlighted with bold arrows. Below is the network diagram for this example,

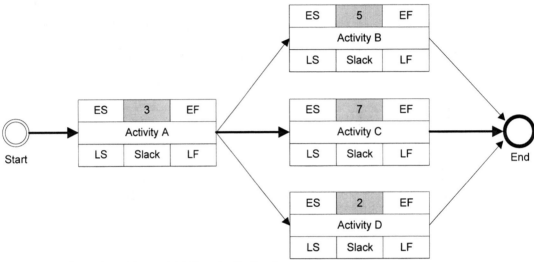

Step 1: Determine ES and EF for Activity A

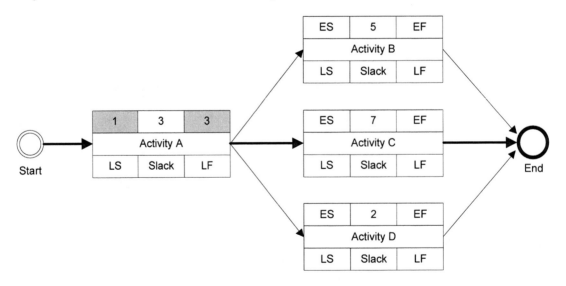

ES = 1

EF = ES + (duration of Activity A) − 1 = 1 + 3 − 1 = 3

Steps 2- 4: Determine ES and EF for Activity B, Activity C and Activity D

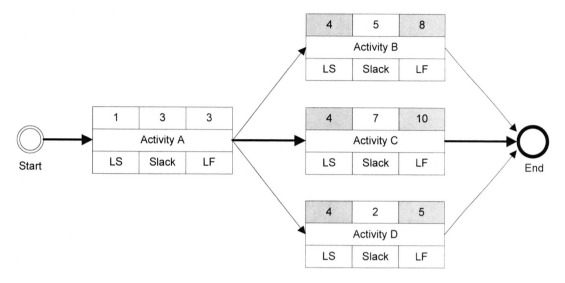

Step 2: Determine ES and EF for Activity B

ES = EF of Activity A + 1 = 3 + 1 = 4

EF = ES + duration of Activity B − 1 = 4 + 5 − 1 = 8

Step 3: Determine ES and EF for Activity C

ES = EF of Activity A + 1 = 3 + 1 = 4

EF = ES + (duration of Activity C) − 1 = 4 + 7 − 1 = 10

Step 4: Determine ES and EF of Activity D

ES = EF of Activity A + 1 = 3 + 1 = 4

EF = ES + (duration of Activity D) − 1 = 4 + 2 − 1 = 5

Steps 5-8: Backward Pass

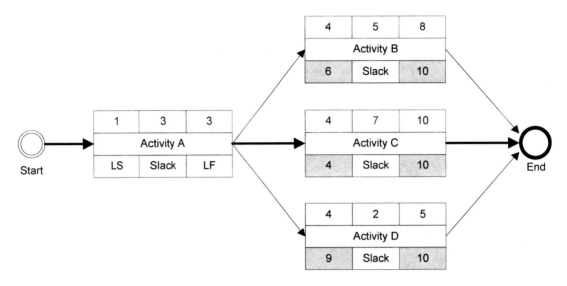

Step 5: Determine LS and LF for Activity B

Activity B's LF should be the same as the EF of the last activity in the critical path. Therefore,

LF for Activity B = EF of Activity C = 10

LS = LF – (duration of Activity B) + 1 = 10 – 5 + 1 = 6

Step 6: Determine LS and LF for Activity C

LF = EF of Activity C = 10

LS = LF – (duration of Activity C) + 1 = 10 – 7 + 1 = 4

Step 7: Determine LS and LF for Activity D

LF = EF of Activity C as it is the last activity in the critical path = 10

LS = LF – (duration of Activity D) + 1 = 10 – 2 + 1 = 9

Step 8: Determine LS and LF for Activity A

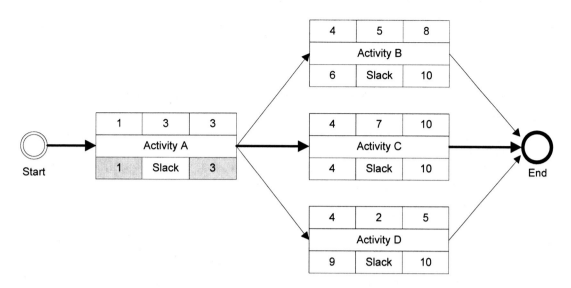

Note that Activity A has 3 successor activities—Activity B, Activity C and Activity D. Thus, LF for Activity A will be (lowest LS among LS of Activity B, LS of Activity C and LS of Activity D) *minus* 1.

LF = (Lowest LS among LS of Activity B, LS of Activity C, and LS of Activity D) – 1 = 4 – 1 = 3

LS = LF – (duration of Activity A) + 1 = 3 – 3 + 1 = 1

Example 4

In this example, we will cover how to determine ES for an activity with multiple predecessor activities.

Below is the network diagram we will use in this example:

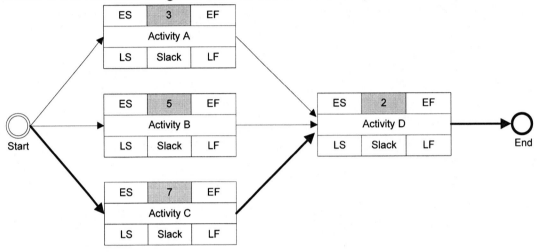

Step 1: Determine Critical Path

First, it will be necessary to identify the paths in the network diagram and total duration for each of the paths.

Path	Total Duration (days)
Start-Activity A-Activity D-End	3 + 2 = 5
Start-Activity B-Activity D-End	5 + 2 = 7
Start-Activity C-Activity D-End	7 + 2 = 9

Based on the total durations computed above, path *Start-Activity C-Activity D-End* is the critical path since it has the highest total duration. The critical path is highlighted with bold arrows.

Steps 2-5: Forward Pass

Steps 2- 4: Determine ES and EF for Activity A, Activity B and Activity C

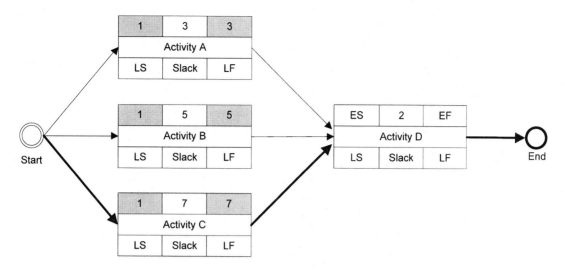

Step 2: Determine ES and EF for Activity A

ES = 1

EF = ES + (duration of Activity A) − 1 = 1 + 3 − 1 = 3

Step 3: Determine ES and EF for Activity B

ES = 1

EF = ES + (duration of Activity B) − 1 = 1 + 5 − 1 = 5

Step 4: Determine ES and EF for Activity C

ES = 1

EF = ES + (duration of Activity C) − 1 = 1 + 7 − 1 = 7

Step 5: Determine ES and EF for Activity D

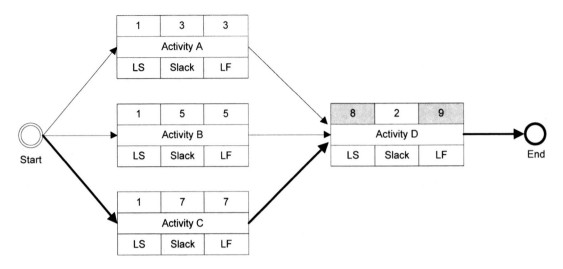

ES = (Highest EF among EF of Activity A, EF of Activity B, and EF of Activity C) + 1 = 7 + 1 = 8

EF = ES + (duration of Activity D) – 1 = 8 + 2 – 1 = 9

Steps 6 – 9: Backward Pass

Step 6: Determine LS and LF for Activity D

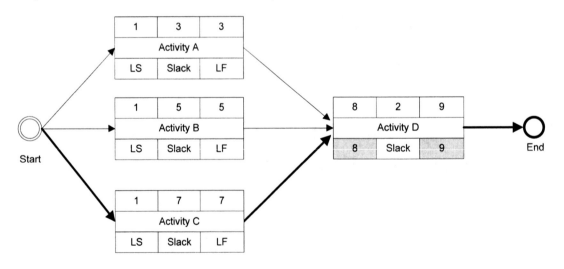

LF = EF of Activity D = 9

LS = LF – (duration of Activity D) + 1 = 9 – 2 + 1 = 8

Steps 7 - 9: Determine LS and LF for Activity A, Activity B and Activity C

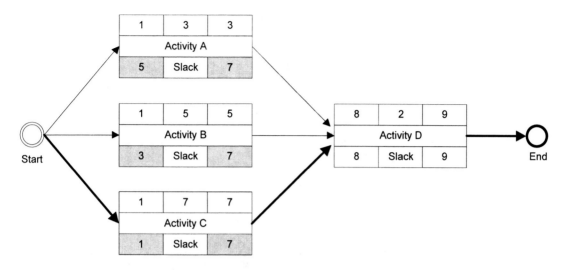

Step 7: Determine LS and LF for Activity A

LF = LS of Activity D – 1 = 8 – 1 = 7

LS = LF – (duration of Activity A) + 1 = 7 – 3 + 1 = 5

Step 8: Determine LS and LF for Activity B

LF = LS of Activity D – 1 = 8 – 1 = 7

LS = LF – (duration of Activity B) + 1 = 7 – 5 + 1 = 3

Step 9: Determine LS and LF for Activity C

LF = LS of Activity D – 1 = 8 – 1 = 7

LS = LF – (duration of Activity C) + 1 = 7 – 7 + 1 = 1

Step 10: Determine Activity Float/Slack

As determined in Step 1, path *Start-Activity C-Activity D-End* is the critical path since it has the highest total duration.

Now, we will determine the slack for each of the activities using the formula: Total duration of critical path *minus* total duration of the path the activity's part of. Note that, since activities C and D are on the critical path, their slack will be 0.

Activity	Slack
A	9 – 5 = 4
B	9 – 7 = 2
C	0
D	0

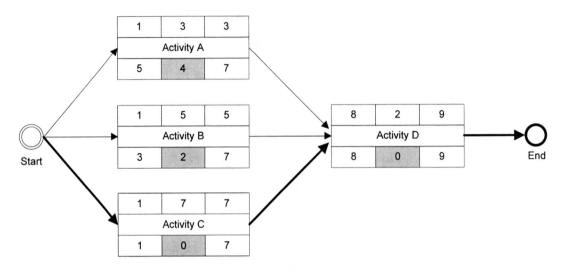

Example 5

In this example network diagram, we have all the 5 activities—Activity A, Activity B, Activity C, Activity D and Activity E—unlike the previous examples.

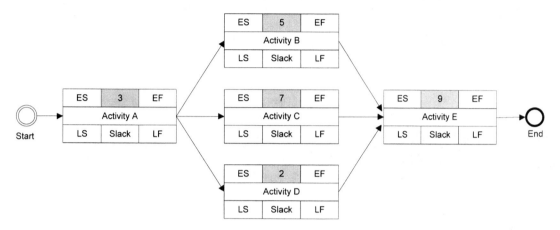

Step 1: Determine ES and EF for Activity A

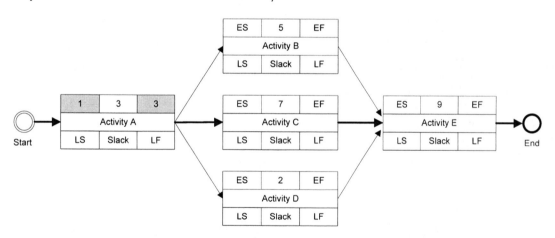

ES = 1

EF = ES + (duration of Activity A) – 1 = 1 + 3 – 1 = 3

Steps 2-4: Determine ES and EF for Activity B, Activity C, and Activity D

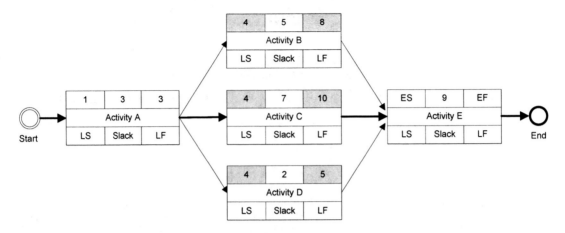

Step 2: Determine ES and EF for Activity B

ES = EF of Activity A + 1 = 4

EF = ES + (duration of Activity B) − 1 = 4 + 5 − 1 = 8

Step 3: Determine ES and EF for Activity C

ES = EF of Activity A + 1 = 3 = 1 = 4

EF = ES + (duration of Activity C) − 1 = 4 + 7 − 1 = 10

Step 4: Determine ES and EF for Activity D

ES = EF of Activity A + 1 = 3 + 1 = 4

EF = ES + (duration of Activity D) − 1 = 4 + 2 − 1 = 5

Step 5: Determine ES and EF for Activity E

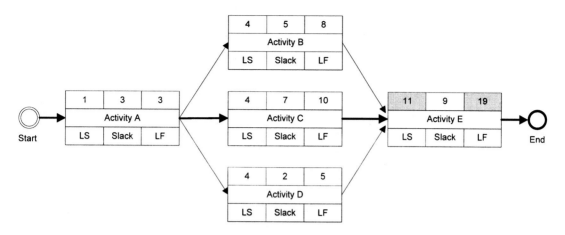

ES = (Highest EF among EF of Activity B, EF of Activity C and EF of Activity D) + 1
= 10 + 1 = 11

EF = ES + (duration of Activity E) – 1 = 11 + 9 – 1 = 19

Steps 6-10: Backward Pass

Step 6: Determine LS and LF for Activity E

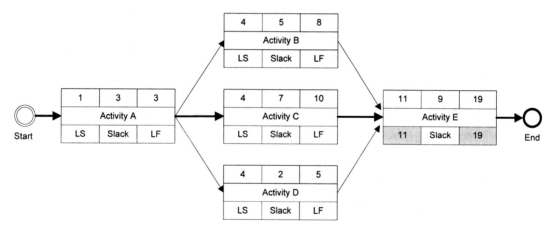

LF = EF of Activity E = 19

LS = LF – (duration of Activity E) + 1 = 19 – 9 + 1 = 11

Steps 7-9: Determine LS and LF for Activity B, Activity C and Activity D

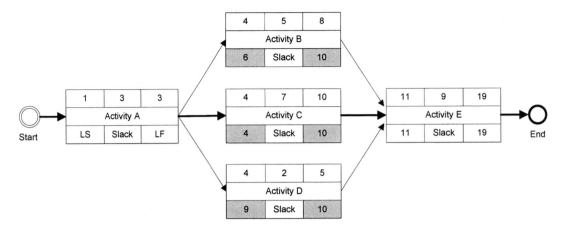

Step 7: Determine LS and LF for Activity B

LF = LS of Activity E – 1 = 11 – 1 = 10

LS = LF – (duration of Activity B) + 1 = 10 – 5 + 1 = 6

Step 8: Determine LS and LF for Activity C

LF = LS of Activity E – 1 = 11 – 1 = 10

LS = LF – (duration of Activity C) + 1 = 10 – 7 + 1 = 4

Step 9: Determine LS and LF for Activity D

LF = LS of Activity E – 1 = 11 – 1 = 10

LS = LF – (duration of Activity D) + 1 = 10 – 2 + 1 = 9

Step 10: Determine LS and LF for Activity A

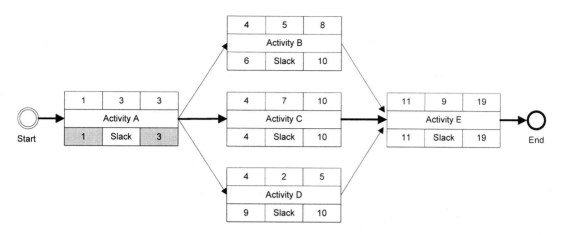

LF = (Lowest LS among LS of Activity B, LS of Activity C, and LS of Activity D) – 1
= 4 – 1 = 3

LS = 3 – 3 + 1 = 1

Determination of each activity slack is left as an exercise using the same steps outlined in previous examples.

Section 5: Conclusion

"I am not sure about project scope but we have
microscopes and telescopes."

Understanding AONs and how CPM can be used to analyze them, covers an important aspect of time management for projects. While there exists software that can be used to create AONs and perform CPM, as a project management professional it is important to know the basic concepts, techniques and how they are applied in order to comprehend and interpret results. Such understanding becomes even more critical when one seeks to create and analyze what-if scenarios. Determining the appropriate and efficient organization of activities including minimizing critical activities and ensuring no-occurrence of negative float or negative total float is an important part of schedule management.

It must also be understood that network diagrams are never static. They can change as project conditions, constraints and other factors change. Project network diagrams can evolve in cases where Rolling Wave Planning is used especially when all project requirements or details are available during the planning phase. Below are benefits that AON and CPM provide for project managers in order to actively, effectively and efficiently manage project schedules.

Knowledge and understanding of the advantages that Activity-On-Node network diagrams bring, along with the use of critical path analysis, is significant in ensuring that they are actually used in management of projects.

Benefits of Using AON and CPM

1. AON provides graphical representation of activity sequence and dependency making it convenient to plan and manage schedule activities. Visual representation makes it easier to communicate the project's activities, their sequence and time attributes.
2. The minimum amount of time required to complete the project can be easily and objectively determined from the network diagram given that the duration of each activity is provided or estimated.
3. Critical Path analysis of a network diagram allows for the identification of critical, near-critical and non-critical activities in the project. Especially for critical activities, it will be easier to determine if there is (are) any threat(s) to the project's completion date.
4. Impact assessments on project schedule can be made for different what-if scenarios. For example, different scenarios can be evaluated to see if

a planned project schedule can be compressed to meet a customer imposed completion date which is earlier than the planned completion date.

5. AONs can be very helpful in tracking project performance with regards to schedule. For instance, delay to an identified critical activity can be immediately identified, and steps can be taken to reduce any threat to the project's completion date.

6. For each activity, the early (start or finish) and late (start or finish) dates can be determined allowing for better schedule management at individual activity level.

7. AONs accommodate all types of logical relationships between activities—FS, FF, SS, SF—including Lags and Leads unlike AOAs which can only use FS (Taylor, 2007).

It is not surprising that no tools and techniques are without disadvantage(s) and limitation(s). One of the frequently cited disadvantages of AONs is the sheer difficulty of constructing it for large complex projects with very large number of activities and dependencies. Hard copy representation of such large network diagrams can be very unwieldy. In addition, use of critical path method on large network diagrams can be cumbersome. Use of software programs that handle creation of network diagrams and critical path analysis can greatly assist in mitigating this disadvantage. The limitation of CPM, which one must have noticed already, is that it relies on the duration of each activity in the network diagram. So, it assumes that the duration of each activity can be relied upon. Therefore, the efficacy of CPM depends heavily on this assumption.

Practice Exercises

1. For the network diagram below, determine the following:
   (a) Critical Path
   (b) ES, EF, LS, LF and Float for each activity

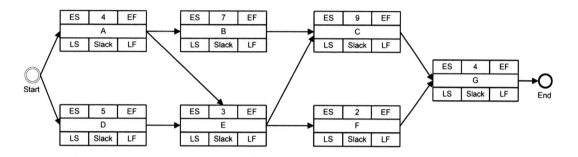

2. For the network diagram below, determine the following:
   (a) Critical Path
   (b) ES, EF, LS, LF and Float for each activity

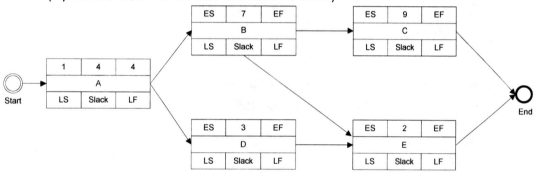

3.

Activity	Predecessor(s)	Duration (days)
A	Start	4
B	A, C, F	7
C	Start	3
D	Start	4
E	B, F	2
F	C	4
G	D, F	9
H	F, G	7
End	E, H	0

Based on the activity details given above, do the following:

    (a) Construct the AON.
    (b) Determine Critical Path
    (c) Determine ES, EF, LS, LF and Float for each activity

4. An activity in a network diagram has an Early Start (ES) of 3 days, Duration of 6 days and Late Finish (LF) of 12 days. What is activity's float?

    (a) 2 days
    (b) 4 days
    (c) 3 days
    (d) 5 days

5. An activity in a network diagram has Duration of 5 days and Early Finish (EF) of 11 days. What is activity's Early Start (ES)?

    (a) 7 days
    (b) 4 days
    (c) 8 days
    (d) 3 days

6. An activity in a network diagram has Duration of 5 days and Late Finish (LF) of 11 days. What is activity's Late Start (LS)?

    (a) 7 days
    (b) 4 days
    (c) 8 days
    (d) 3 days

7. An activity in a network diagram has Duration of 5 days and Late Start (LS) of 3 days. What is activity's Late Finish (LF)?

    (a) 7 days
    (b) 4 days
    (c) 8 days
    (d) 3 days

8. A landscaper must complete preparing the flower bed before the flower plants can be planted. The relationship between "prepare flower bed" activity and "plant flower plants" can be best described as:

(a) Start-Finish (SF)
(b) Finish-Start (FS)
(c) Finish-Finish (FF)
(d) Start-Start (SS)

9. A homeowner plans to sealcoat the driveway of his house. He has already purchased the required quantity of driveway seal coater and the weather would be right to do it. The seal coating material dries quickly and therefore, must be spread without delay. He has already washed and cleaned his driveway, and is prepared to start sealcoating the driveway. Next day, he knows he has to primarily perform two activities—pour the seal coater, and spread the sealcoater. The relationship between the predecessor activity to pour the sealcoater and the successor activity to spread the seal coater can be best described as:
   (a) Start-Finish (SF)
   (b) Finish-Start (FS)
   (c) Finish-Finish (FF)
   (d) Start-Start (SS)

10. At a trade show, two teams were employed to set up electric connection and lighting for each booth. One team laid out the electric cables and connection while the other team set up the lighting and made sure it was set up as per specifications. Both teams must ensure that they have fully completed before the scheduled start date. The relationship between the two teams activities can be best described as:
   (a) Start-Finish (SF)
   (b) Finish-Start (FS)
   (c) Finish-Finish (FF)
   (d) Start-Start (SS)

Further Readings

Angel, George G. *PMP Certification, A Beginner's Guide*. The McGraw-Hill Companies, 2010.

Crowe, Andy. *The PMP Exam: How to Pass on Your First Try*. Kennesaw, Georgia: Velociteach, 2009.

Glenwright Jr., Earl T. *Let's Scrap the Precedence Diagramming Method*. AACE International Transactions, 2004.

Greene, Jennifer, Andrew Stellman. *Head First PMP: A Brain-Friendly Guide to Passing the Project Management Professional Exam*. Sebastopol, California: O'Reilly Media, 2009.

Heldman, Kim, Claudia M. Baca, Patti M. Jansen. *PMP Project Management Professional Exam Study Guide*. Sybex, 2007.

Mulcahy, Rita. *PMP® Exam Prep*. RMC Publications, Inc., 2002.

Newell, Michael W. *Preparing for the Project Management Professional (PMP®) Certification Exam*, 2nd Edition. New York, New York: AMACOM, 2002.

Phillips, Joseph. *Project Management Professional Study Guide*. 3rd Edition. The McGraw-Hill Companies, 2010.

Portny, Stanley E. *Project Management for Dummies*. Hoboken, NJ: The Wiley Publishing, 2010.

Project Management Institute. *A Guide to the Project Management Body of Knowledge (PMBOK Guide)*. Fourth Edition. Newtown Square, Pennsylvania: Project Management Institute, 2008.

Subramanian, Vidya, Ravi Ramachandran. *McGraw-Hill's PMP Certification Mathematics with CD-ROM*. McGraw-Hill, 2010.

Taylor, James. *Project Scheduling and Cost Control: Planning, Monitoring and Controlling the Baseline*. Fort Lauderdale, Florida: J. Ross Publishing, 2007.

Wysocki, Robert K. *Effective Project Management: Traditional, Agile, Extreme*. 5th Edition. Indianapolis, Indiana: The Wiley Publishing, 2009.

Solutions

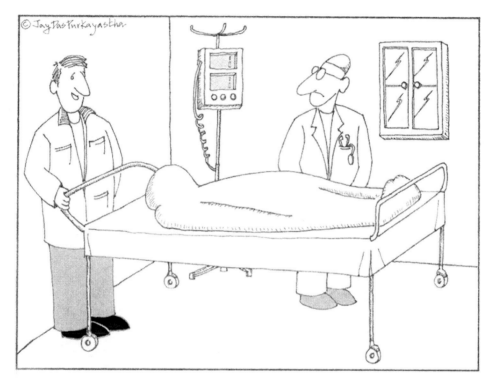

"Doc, is this the last possible solution you had mentioned?"

Note:

> The solutions to exercises 1, 2 and 3 use the Total Path Duration in determining Critical Path(s) in a project network diagram. Reader is advised to use the Activity Float approach as an exercise to determine Critical Paths for the same exercises.

1.

(a) In order to determine the critical path, i.e. the path with the longest duration in the network diagram let us first identify and list each of the network paths. Then we determine the total duration of each path by summing the duration of each activity in the path. In the final step, we compare the total duration of the paths in order to determine the path with the highest duration and this path is the critical path.

Step 1: The paths in the network diagram are:

1. Start-A-B-C-G-End

2. Start-D-E-F-G-End

3. Start-A-E-F-G-End

4. Start-A-E-C-G-End

5. Start-D-E-C-G-End

Step 2: Determine the total duration of each of the paths identified in Step 1.

Path	Total Duration (days)
Start-A-B-C-G-End	4 + 7 + 9 + 4 = 24
Start-D-E-F-G-End	5 + 3 + 2 + 4 = 14
Start-A-E-F-G-End	4 + 3 + 2 + 4 = 13
Start-A-E-C-G-End	4 + 3 + 9 + 4 = 20
Start-D-E-C-G-End	5 + 3 + 9 + 4 = 21

Based on the total durations computed above, path *Start-A-B-C-G-End* is the critical path since it has the highest total duration.

(b) For this section, we will do the steps for Forward Pass first to determine early start and finish times for each activity in the network diagram, and then we will use Backward Pass to determine late start and finish times for the same activities.

Forward Pass Steps:

Step 1: Determine ES and EF for activity A and activity D

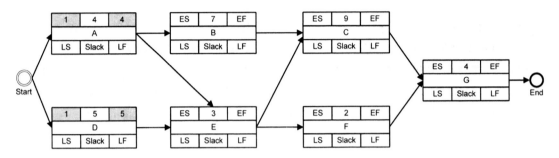

For activity A:

$ES_A = 1$

$EF_A = ES_A +$ (duration of activity A) $- 1 = 1 + 4 - 1 = 4$

For activity D:

$ES_D = 1$

$EF_D = ES_D +$ (duration of activity D) $- 1 = 1 + 5 - 1 = 5$

Step 2: Determine ES and EF for Activity B

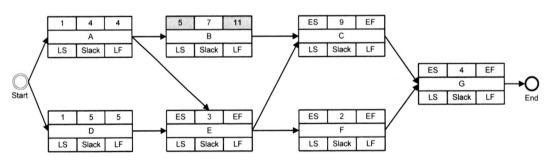

$ES_B = EF_A + 1 = 4 + 1 = 5$

$EF_B = ES_B + $ (duration of activity B) $- 1 = 5 + 7 - 1 = 11$

Step 3: Determine ES and EF for activity E

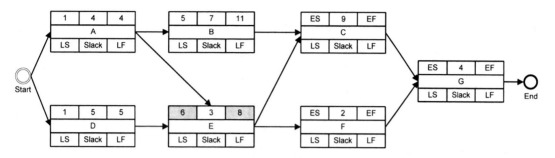

$ES_E = $ (Highest EF among EF of activity A and EF of activity D) $+ 1 = 5 + 1 = 6$

$EF_E = ES_E + $ (duration of activity E) $- 1 = 6 + 3 - 1 = 8$

Step 4: Determine ES and EF of activity C

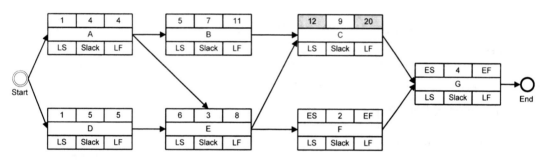

$ES_C = $ (Highest EF among EF of activity B and EF of activity E) $+ 1 = EF_B + 1 = 11 + 1 = 12$

$EF_C = ES_C + $ (duration of activity C) $- 1 = 12 + 9 - 1 = 20$

Step 5: Determine ES and EF of activity F

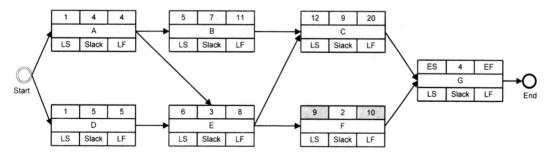

$ES_F = EF_E + 1 = 8 + 1 = 9$

$EF_F = ES_F + (\text{duration of activity F}) - 1 = 9 + 2 - 1 = 10$

Step 6: Determine ES and EF of activity G

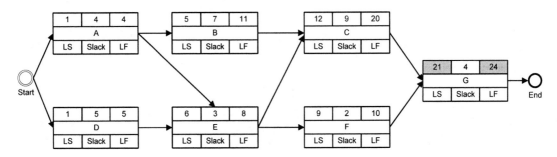

$ES_G = (\text{Highest EF among EF of activity C and EF of activity F}) + 1 = 20 + 1 = 21$

$EF_G = ES_G + (\text{duration of activity G}) - 1 = 21 + 4 - 1 = 24$

Now, we will be using Backward Pass to determine LF and LS for each of the activities.

Step 7: Determine LS and LF for activity G

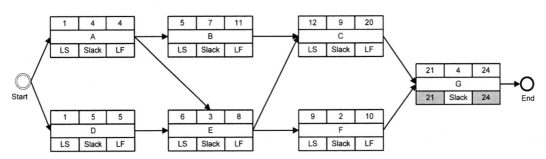

$LF_G = EF_G = 24$

$LS_G = LF_G - (\text{duration of activity G}) + 1 = 24 - 4 + 1 = 21$

Step 8: Determine LS and LF for activity F

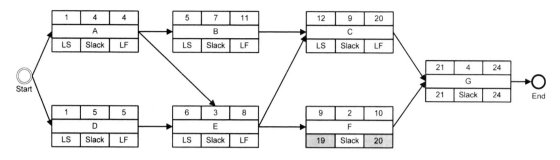

$LF_F = LS_G - 1 = 21 - 1 = 20$

$LS_F = LF_F - (\text{duration of activity F}) + 1 = 20 - 2 + 1 = 19$

Step 9: Determine LS and LF for activity C

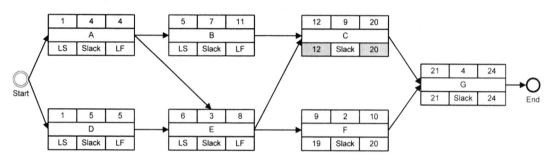

$LF_C = LS_G - 1 = 21 - 1 = 20$

$LS_C = LF_C - (\text{duration of activity C}) + 1 = 20 - 9 + 1 = 12$

Step 10: Determine LS and LF for activity B

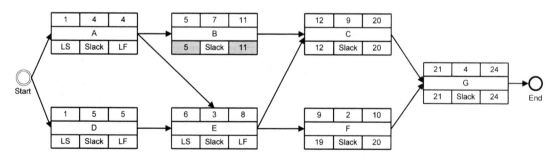

$LF_B = LS_C - 1 = 12 - 1 = 11$

$LS_B = LF_B - (\text{duration of activity B}) + 1 = 11 - 7 + 1 = 5$

Step 11: Determine LS and LF for activity A

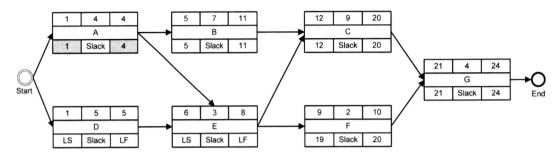

$LF_A = LS_B - 1 = 5 - 1 = 4$

$LS_A = LF_A - (\text{duration of activity A}) + 1 = 4 - 4 + 1 = 1$

Step 12: Determine LS and LF for activity E

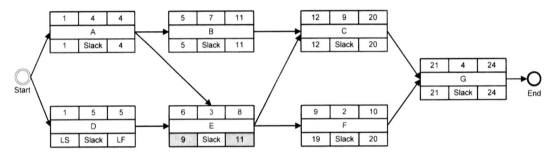

$LF_E = (\text{Lowest LS among LS of activity C and LS of activity F}) - 1 = 12 - 1 = 11$

$LS_E = LF_E - (\text{duration of activity E}) + 1 = 11 - 3 + 1 = 9$

Step 13: Determine LS and LF of activity D

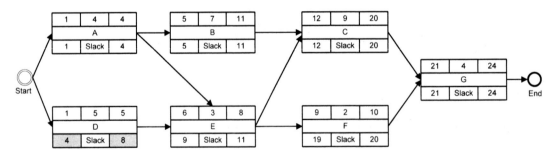

$LF_D = LS_E - 1 = 9 - 1 = 8$

$LS_D = LF_D - (\text{duration of activity E}) + 1 = 8 - 5 + 1 = 4$

Step 14: Determine Float/Slack for all activities

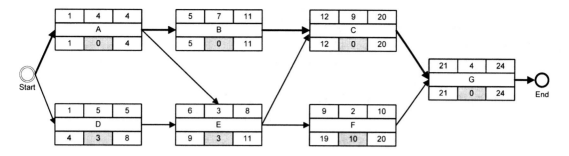

Now, we will determine the slack for each of the activities.

Activity	Slack	Comments
A	0	As it is on critical path.
B	0	As it is on critical path.
C	0	As it is on critical path.
D	3	Difference between critical path duration and path with the highest duration among all the paths activity D is in.
E	3	Difference between critical path duration and path with the highest duration among all the paths that activity E is in.
F	10	Difference between critical path duration and path with the highest duration among all the paths that activity F is in.
G	0	As it is on critical path.

Since the critical path is *Start-A-B-C-G-End*, all the activities in the network diagram are critical activities. Therefore, the slack or float of each of the critical activities is 0.

2.

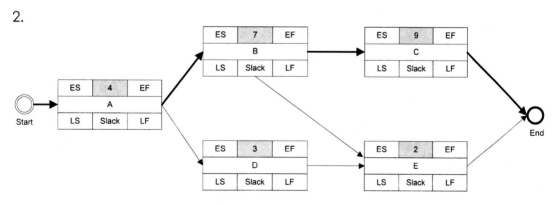

(a) In order to determine the critical path, i.e. the path with the longest duration in the network diagram let us first identify and list each of the network paths. Then we will determine the total duration of each path by summing the duration of each activity in the path. In the final step, we will compare the total duration of the paths in order to determine the path with the highest duration and this path would be the critical path.

Step 1: The paths in the network diagram are:

Start-A-B-C-End

Start-A-B-E-End

Start-A-D-E-End

Step 2: Determine the total duration of each of the paths identified in Step 1.

Path	Total Duration (days)
Start-A-B-C-End	4 + 7 + 9 = 20
Start-A-B-E-End	4 + 7 + 2 = 13
Start-A-D-E-End	4 + 3 + 2 = 9

Based on the total durations computed above, path *Start-A-B-C-End* is the critical path since it has the highest total duration.

(b) For this section, we will do the steps for Forward Pass first to determine early start and finish times for each activity in the network diagram, and then we will use Backward Pass to determine late start and finish times for the same activities.

Forward Pass Steps:

Step 1: Determine ES and EF for activity A

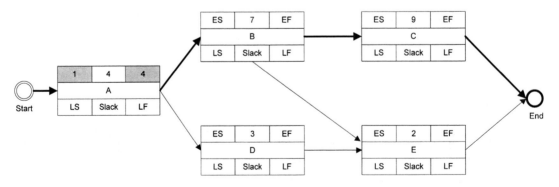

$ES_A = 1$

$EF_A = ES_A +$ (duration of Activity A) $- 1 = 1 + 4 - 1 = 4$

Step 2: Determine ES and EF for Activity B

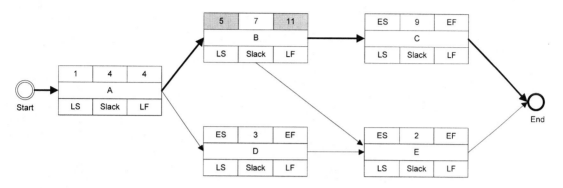

$ES_B = EF_A + 1 = 4 + 1 = 5$

$EF_B = ES_B +$ (duration of Activity B) $- 1 = 5 + 7 - 1 = 11$

Step 3: Determine ES and EF of Activity C

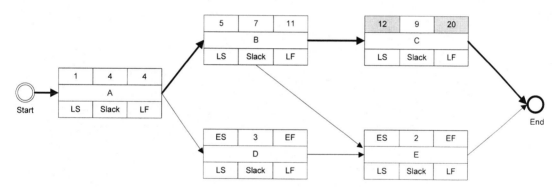

$ES_C = EF_B + 1 = 11 + 1 = 12$

$EF_C = ES_C +$ (duration of Activity C) $- 1 = 12 + 9 - 1 = 20$

Step 4: Determine ES and EF of Activity D

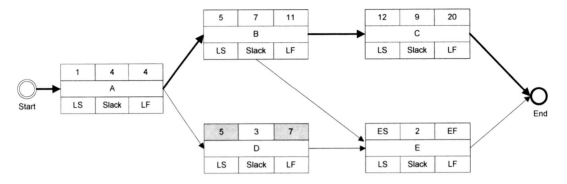

ES_D = EF of activity A + 1 = EF_A + 1 = 4 + 1 = 5

EF_D = ES_D + (duration of activity D) – 1 = 5 + 3 – 1 = 7

Step 5: Determine ES and EF of Activity E

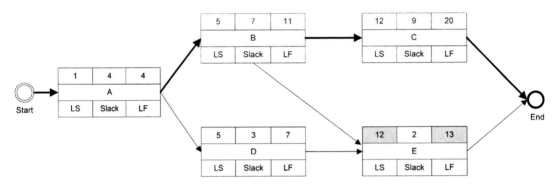

ES_E = (Highest EF among EF of activity B and EF of activity D) + 1 = EF_B + 1 = 11 + 1 = 12

EF_E = ES_E + (duration of activity E) – 1 = 12 + 2 – 1 = 13

Now, we will be using Backward Pass to determine LF and LS for each of the activities.

Step 6: Determine LS and LF for activity C and activity E

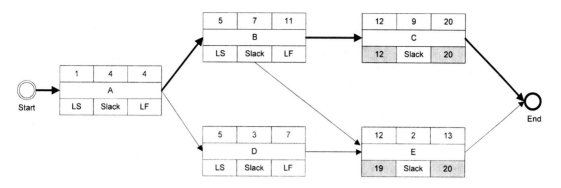

Activity C:

LF_C = EF of last activity in the critical path = EF_C = 20

$LS_C = LF_C$ – (duration of activity C) + 1 = 20 – 9 + 1 = 12

Activity E:

LF_E = EF of last activity in the critical path = EF_C = 20

$LS_E = LF_E$ – (duration of activity E) + 1 = 20 – 2 + 1 = 19

Step 7: Determine LS and LF for activity D

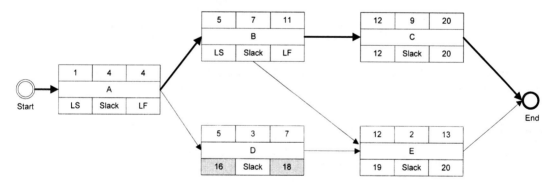

$LF_D = LS_E – 1 = 19 – 1 = 18$

$LS_D = LF_D$ – (duration of activity D) + 1 = 18 – 3 + 1 = 16

Step 8: Determine LS and LF for activity B

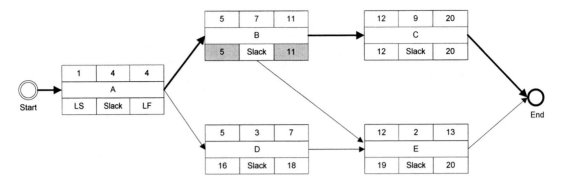

LF_B = (Lowest LS among LS of activity C and LS of activity E) - 1= LS_C - 1= 11

LS_B = LF_B – (duration of Activity B) + 1 = 11 – 7 + 1 = 5

Step 9: Determine LS and LF for activity A

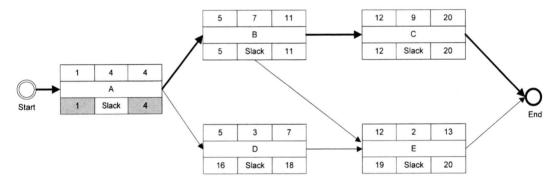

LF_A = (Lowest LS among LS of activity B and LS of activity D) – 1 = LS_B – 1 = 5 – 1 = 4

LS_A = LF_A – (duration of activity A) + 1 = 4 – 4 + 1 = 1

Step 10: Determine the slack for each of the activities

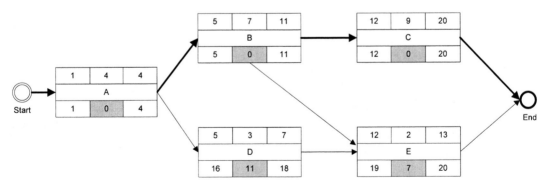

Since the critical path is *Start-A-B-C-End*, all the activities in the network diagram are critical activities. Therefore, the slack or float of each of the critical activities is 0.

Activity	Slack	Comments
A	0	As it is on critical path.
B	0	As it is on critical path.
C	0	As it is on critical path.
D	11	Difference between critical path duration and path with activity D is in.
E	7	Difference between critical path duration and path with the highest duration among all the paths that activity E is in.

3.

Activity	Predecessor(s)	Duration (days)
A	Start	4
B	A, C, F	7
C	Start	3
D	Start	4
E	B, F	2
F	C	4
G	D, F	9
H	F, G	7
End	E, H	0

(a) The Activity-On-Node (AON) diagram constructed using Precedence Diagramming Method (PDM) is below along with the provided duration of each activity:

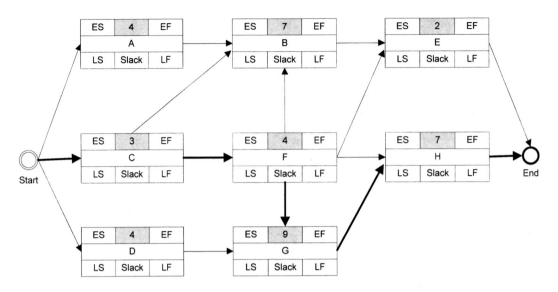

(b) In order to determine the critical path, i.e. the path with the longest duration in the network diagram, let's first identify and list each of the network paths. Then, we will determine the total duration of each path by summing the duration of each activity in the path. In the final step, we will compare the total duration of the paths in order to determine the path with the highest duration, and this path would be the critical path.

The paths in the network diagram are:

Path	Total Duration (days)
Start-A-B-E-End	4 + 7 + 2 = 13
Start-C-F-H-End	3 + 4 + 7 = 14
Start-C-B-E-End	3 + 7 + 2 = 12
Start-D-G-H-End	4 + 9 + 7 = 20
Start-C-F-B-E-End	3 + 4 + 7 + 2 = 16
Start-C-F-G-H-End	3 + 4 + 9 + 7 = 23
Start-C-F-E-End	3 + 4 + 2 = 9

Based on the total durations computed above, path *Start-C-F-G-H-End* is the critical path since it has the highest total duration.

(c) For this section, we will do the steps for Forward Pass first to determine early start and finish times for each activity in the network diagram, and then we will use Backward Pass to determine late start and finish times for the same activities.

Forward Pass Steps:

Step 1: Determine ES and EF for activities A, C and D

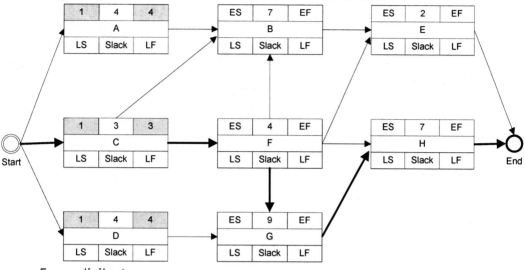

For activity A:

$ES_A = 1$

$EF_A = ES_A + $ (duration of activity A) $- 1 = 1 + 4 - 1 = 4$

For activity C:

$ES_C = 1$

$EF_C = ES_C + $ (duration of activity C) $- 1 = 1 + 3 - 1 = 3$

For activity D:

$ES_D = 1$

$EF_D = ES_D + $ (duration of activity D) $- 1 = 1 + 4 - 1 = 4$

Step 2: Determine ES and EF for activity F

Note:

ES and EF for activity F are determined before ES and EF for activity B because activity F is a predecessor to activity B and EF of activity F along with EFs of activity A and activity C will be required in order to determine ES of activity B.

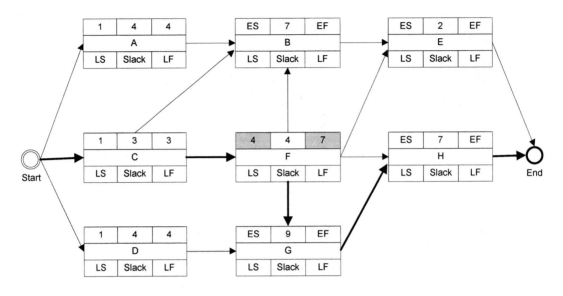

$ES_F = EF_C + 1 = 3 + 1 = 4$

$EF_F = ES_F + (\text{duration of activity F}) - 1 = 4 + 4 - 1 = 7$

Step 3: Determine ES and EF for activity G

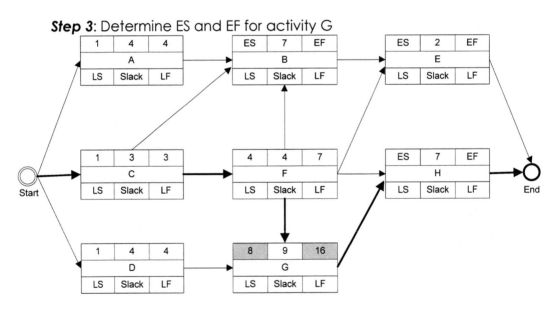

$ES_G = (\text{Highest EF among EF of activity F and EF of activity D}) + 1 = EF_F + 1 = 7 + 1 = 8$

$EF_G = ES_G + (\text{duration of activity G}) - 1 = 8 + 9 - 1 = 16$

Step 4: Determine ES and EF for activity B

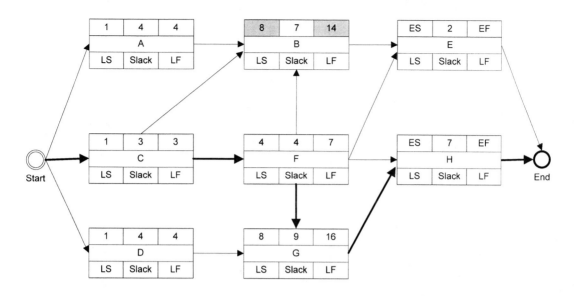

ES_B = (Highest EF among EF of activities A, C and F) + 1 = EF_F + 1 = 7 + 1 = 8

EF_B = ES_B + (duration of activity B) – 1 = 8 + 7 – 1 = 14

Step 5: ES and EF for activity E

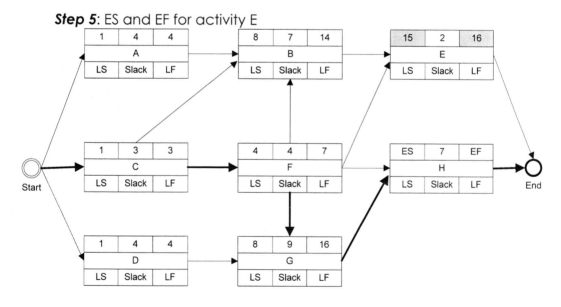

ES_E = (Highest EF among EF of activities B and F) + 1 = EF_B + 1 = 14 + 1 = 15

EF_E = ES_E + (duration of activity E) – 1 = 15 + 2 - 1 = 16

Step 6: Determine ES and EF for activity H

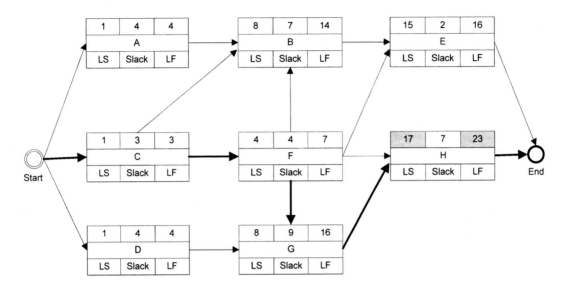

ES_H = (Highest EF among activities F and G) + 1 = EF_G + 1 = 16 + 1 = 17
EF_H = ES_H + duration of activity H – 1 = 17 + 7 – 1 = 23

Now, we will be using Backward Pass to determine LF and LS for each of the activities.

Step 7: Determine LF and LS for activity H

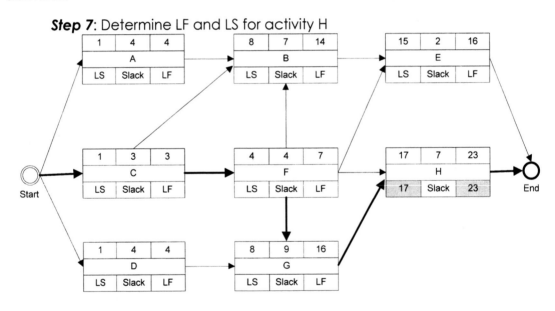

LF_H = EF of last activity in the critical path = EF_H = 23
LS_H = LF_H – (duration of activity H) + 1 = 23 – 7 + 1 = 17

Step 8: Determine LF and LS for activity E

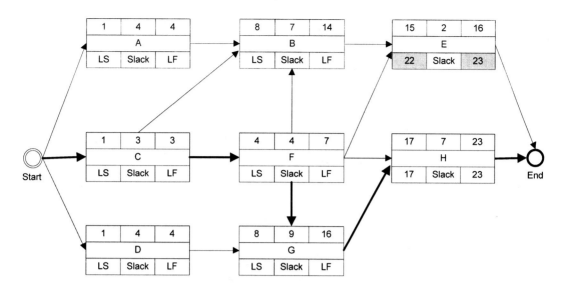

LF_E = LF of last activity in the critical path = LF_H = 23
LF_E = LF of last activity in the critical path = LF_H = 23
LS_E = LF_E − (duration of activity E) + 1 = 23 − 2 + 1 = 22

Step 9: Determine LF and LS of activity B

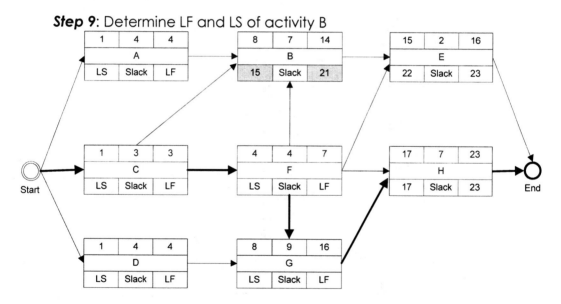

LF_B = LS_E − 1 = 22 − 1 = 21. **Note**: *LS of activity E is used as activity E is the only successor activity for activity B.*
LS_B = LF_B − (duration of activity B) + 1 = 21 − 7 + 1 = 15

Step 10: Determine LF and LS of activity G

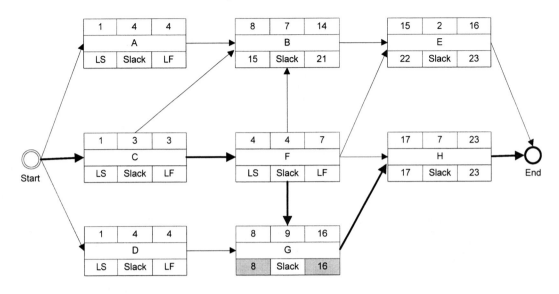

$LF_G = LS_H - 1 = 17 - 1 = 16$
$LS_G = LF_G - \text{(duration of activity G)} + 1 = 16 - 9 + 1 = 8$

Step 11: Determine LF and LS of activity F

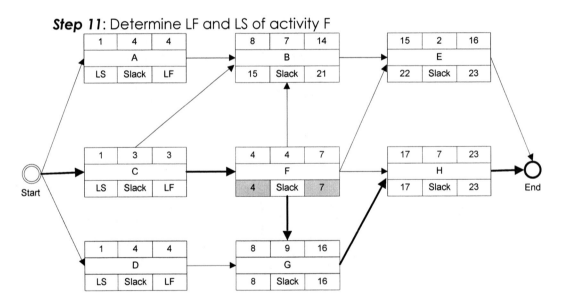

$LF_F = \text{(Lowest of LS of activity E, activity H, activity B, and activity G)} - 1 = LS_G - 1 = 8 - 1 = 7$
$LS_F = LF_F - \text{(duration of activity F)} + 1 = 7 - 4 + 1 = 4$

Step 12: Determine LF and LS of activity D

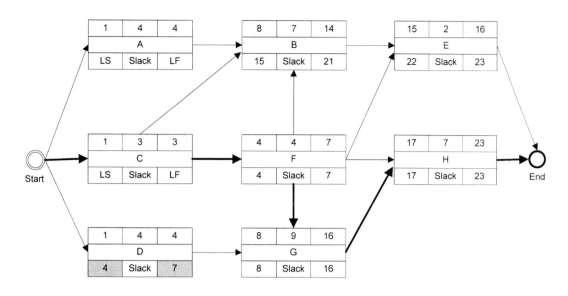

$LF_D = LS_G - 1 = 8 - 1 = 7$
$LS_D = LF_D - (\text{duration of activity D}) + 1 = 7 - 4 + 1 = 4$

Step 13: Determine LF and LS of activity C

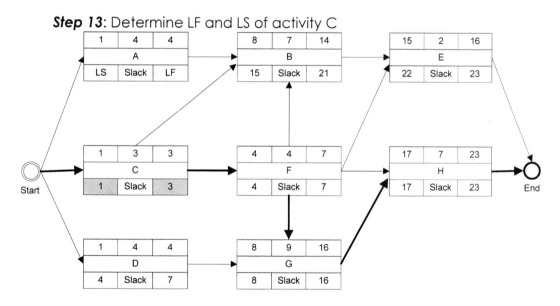

$LF_C = (\text{Lowest LS of activity B and activity F}) - 1 = LS_F - 1 = 4 - 1 = 3$
$LS_C = LF_C - (\text{duration of activity C}) + 1 = 3 - 3 + 1 = 1$

Step 14: Determine LF and LS of activity A

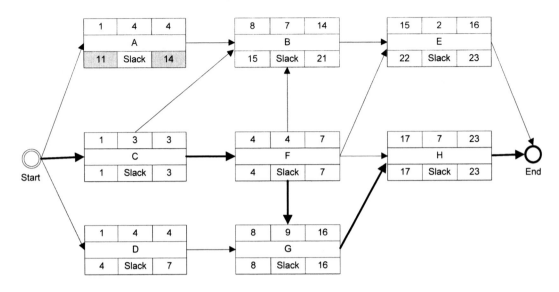

$LF_A = LS_B - 1 = 15 - 1 = 14$

$LS_A = LF_A - (duration\ of\ activity\ A) + 1 = 14 - 4 + 1 = 11$

Step 15: Determine Float/Slack for each of the activities

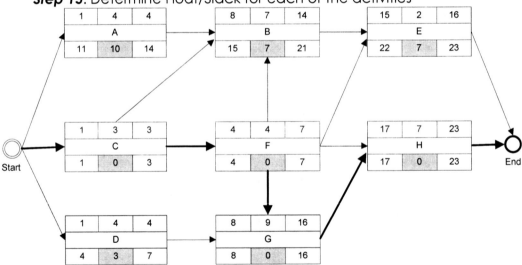

The slack for an activity can be determined by taking the difference of the critical path duration and the path the activity is on. If the activity is on multiple non-critical paths, then take the difference between the critical path duration and the path with the activity having highest total duration so that the least possible slack for the activity is obtained.

Activity	Slack
A	10
B	7
C	0
D	3
E	7
F	0
G	0
H	0

Since the critical path is *Start-C-F-G-H-End*, all the activities in the network diagram are critical activities. Therefore, the slack or float of each of the critical activities is 0.

4. Correct answer: (b)
   Explanation:
   It is given, ES = 3 days and duration = 6 days
   Early Finish (EF) = ES + duration − 1 = 3 + 6 − 1 = 8 days
   Float = Late Finish (LF) *minus* Early Finish (EF) = 12 − 8 = 4 days

5. Correct answer: (a)
   Explanation:
   It is given, EF = 11 days and duration = 5 days
   Early Finish (EF) = ES + duration − 1 = ES + 5 − 1 = ES + 4
   ⇨ 11 = ES + 4
   ⇨ ES = 11 − 4 = 7 days

6. Correct answer: (a)
   Explanation:
   It is given, LF = 11 days and duration = 5 days
   Late Start (LS) = LF - duration + 1 = 11 - 5 + 1 = 7 days

7. Correct answer: (a)
   Explanation:
   It is given, LS = 3 days and duration = 5 days
   Late Start (LS) = LF - duration + 1
   ⇨ 3 = LF − 5 + 1
   ⇨ 3 = LF − 4
   ⇨ LF = 7 days

8. Correct answer: (b)

Explanation:
Activity "prepare flower bed", which is a predecessor activity for "plant flower plants" activity, must be complete, i.e. finished before the successor activity—"plant flower plants"—can start, and clearly shows that the relationship is Finish-Start (FS).

9. Correct answer: (d)
Explanation:
Activity "spread the seal coater" cannot start until "pouring of the seal coater" activity starts. Pouring the sealcoating is a preceding activity and spreading the sealcoating is a successor activity. However, as the seal coater can dry quickly, spreading of the seal coater must start along with the start of the pouring of the seal coater. This relationship can be best described as Start-Start (SS).

10. Correct answer: (c)
Explanation: The team that lays out the electric wiring and sets up connections must do it for each booth in the trade show. Likewise, the other team must set up lighting as per specifications for each booth which the other team has already wired and provided connection. It is not important when each team started their respective activities. However, it is important that they finish prior to the scheduled start day for the trade show. Both teams are not expected to finish at the same time. In fact, the team laying out the electric wiring must finish before the other team can set up the lighting. The dependency between the two teams' activities is Finish-Finish (FF).

Index

A

Activity-on-Arrow.................... *3*, *15*
Activity-On-Node *3*, *5*, *6*, *15*
ADM.......*See* Arrow Diagramming Method
AOA .... *See* Activity-on-Arrow
AON .... *See* Activity-On-Node
Arrow Diagramming Method. *3*, *5*, *15*

B

Backward Pass ... *6*, *33*, *37*, *38*, *78*, *84*, *86*, *91*

C

CPM ......*See* Critical Path Method
Critical Activities *6*, *25*
critical activity *25*
critical path.. *14*, *25*, *26*, *33*, *77*, *83*, *84*, *89*, *90*, *98*, *99*
Critical Path .. *14*, *See* critical path
Critical Path Method .. *3*, *5*, *23*, *25*, *33*

D

Duration.. *6*, *8*, *9*, *10*, *12*, *25*, *30*, *71*, *77*, *84*, *89*, *90*

E

Early Finish ... *6*, *9*, *10*, *11*, *12*, *14*, *33*
Early Start..... *6*, *9*, *10*, *11*, *12*, *14*, *33*
EF............................*See* Early Finish
Effort... *8*, *9*
ES............................... *See* Early Start

F

FF............................*See* Finish-Finish
Finish Float *11*, *12*
Finish-Finish *6*, *15*, *17*, *18*
Finish-Start *6*, *15*, *16*, *17*
Finish-to-Finish ....*See* Finish-Finish
Finish-to-Start..........*See* Finish-Start
Float........................*6*, *10*, *25*, *71*, *72*
Forward Pass...*6*, *33*, *34*, *38*, *78*, *84*, *90*, *91*
Free Float *10*, *15*
FS...........................*See* Finish-Start

H

Hypercritical.............................*6*, *25*

L

Lag...*6*, *21*
Late Finish.........*6*, *10*, *11*, *12*, *14*, *37*
Late Start *6*, *9*, *10*, *11*, *12*, *14*, *37*, *38*
Lead *6*, *22*
LF............................ *See* Late Finish
LS.............................*See* Late Start

N

Near-Critical Activities *25*
Near-Critical Paths *25*
Negative Float............................*14*
Network Path..............................*25*

P

PDM .... *See* Precedence Diagramming Method

Precedence Diagramming
Method *3, 6, 15, 74, 89*
Project Float...............................*14*

S

SF............................ *See Start-Finish*
Slack......................*6, 10, 83, 89, 99*
SS...........................*See Start-Start*
Start Float..............................*11, 12*
Start-Finish *6, 15, 18, 19*
Start-Start *6, 15, 19*
Start-to-Finish .... *See Start-Finish*

Start-to-Start.............*See Start-Start*
Supercritical................................*25*

T

Total Float *12, 15, 25*

W

WBS..............*See Work Breakdown*
Structure
Work Breakdown Structure *6*
work package..............................*6*
work package element...............*6*

CPSIA information can be obtained at www.ICGtesting.com
Printed in the USA
LVOW131649290312

275322LV00005B/50/P